Making the Most of

U N D E R S T A N D I N G

by D E S I G N

John L. Brown

Association for Supervision and Curriculum Development
Alexandria, Virginia USA

Association for Supervision and Curriculum Development
1703 N. Beauregard St. • Alexandria, VA 22311-1714 USA
Telephone: 800-933-2723 or 703-578-9600 • Fax: 703-575-5400
Web site: http://www.ascd.org • E-mail: member@ascd.org

Gene R. Carter, *Executive Director*; Nancy Modrak, *Director of Publishing*; Julie Houtz, *Director of Book Editing & Production*; Katie Martin, *Project Manager*; Shelley Young, *Senior Graphic Designer*; BMWW, *Typesetter*; Tracey Smith, *Production Manager*.

s4/04

Paperback ISBN: 0-87120-860-1 • ASCD product #103110 • List Price: $24.95
($19.95 ASCD member price, direct from ASCD only)
e-books ($24.95): netLibrary ISBN 0-87120-998-8 • ebrary ISBN 0-87120-989-6

Library of Congress Cataloging-in-Publication Data

Brown, John L., 1947–
  Making the most of Understanding by design / John L. Brown.
    p. cm.
  Includes bibliographical references and index.
  ISBN 0-87120-860-1 (print : alk. paper) — ISBN 0-87120-988-8 (netlibrary ebook) — ISBN 0-87120-989-6 (ebrary ebook)
  1. Wiggins, Grant P., 1950– Understanding by design. 2. Curriculum planning—United States. 3. Curriculum-based assessment—United States. 4. Learning. 5. Comprehension. I. Wiggins, Grant P., 1950– Understanding by design. II. Title.

  LB2806.15.B77 2004
  375'.001—dc22

                                                          2004000854

11 10 09 08 07 06 05 04   12 11 10 9 8 7 6 5 4 3 2

Making the Most of

U N D E R S T A N D I N G

by D E S I G N

FIGURES

Foreword

■ ■ ■

Understanding by Design (UbD) presents a framework for curriculum design oriented toward the development and deepening of student understanding of "big ideas" in content areas. It is *not* a program with an articulated "scope and sequence" of skills or prescribed teaching activities. Thus, it becomes challenging to unearth direct, causal evidence of its effectiveness on student achievement. Nevertheless, the growing use of the UbD framework demands empirical data to guide users and document its effects.

Making the Most of Understanding by Design begins this needed research journey. John L. Brown offers a rich description of UbD users' experiences compiled from extensive surveys. The surveys' findings reflect the "lessons learned" from multiple perspectives, including those of teachers, school-based administrators, district-level supervisors, staff developers, regional service agency staff, and personnel from higher education. The results of the surveys and follow-up telephone interviews are described in richly detailed narratives, supplemented by numerous charts and tables. However, the book provides more than a thorough presentation of data. It offers a synthesis of underlying patterns to guide users in recognizing the most promising practices, highlighting predictable pitfalls to avoid, and raising questions for further research.

While there is no single pathway to UbD implementation, Brown's research reveals that some actions have proven more robust than others. The insights provided in this book will benefit both veteran and novice users of Understanding by Design.

Jay McTighe and Grant Wiggins

Preface

■   ■   ■

In the groundbreaking publication *The Fifth Discipline: The Art and Practice of the Learning Organization* (1990), Peter M. Senge characterizes a "learning organization" as one that demonstrates "metanoia," a capacity for self-reflection and self-examination that results in stakeholders' continuous learning and, in turn, the organization's continuous improvement. Through a commitment to sustained self-evaluation and self-modification based on analysis of achievement data, a learning organization's members can successfully discover what Senge (1990, p. 114) labels "points of leverage"—areas where organizational emphasis can produce the most significant and positive results.

Ideally, both schools and school districts should embody Senge's concept of the learning organization. In light of growing public demand for rigorous standards, accountability-based assessments, and high achievement levels for all students, educators are continually searching for models, frameworks, and exemplars to improve their delivery of services and to develop metanoia, either consciously or unconsciously. This book provides a road map that educators, parents, and community members can use to examine the continuous improvement implications of one such framework, Understanding by Design (UbD) by Grant Wiggins and Jay McTighe.

The data underlying this book emerged from a study organized by the UbD cadre, a group of educators throughout the United States and Canada who work closely with Wiggins and McTighe to ensure quality control of all aspects of Understanding by Design–related professional development, strategic planning, and publishing. Members of the cadre represent ASCD-certified training experts who have extensive experience in curriculum, assessment, instruction, and administration. They represent a wide range of professional settings and responsibilities (from elementary, middle, and high schools to central office and university venues) and reflect a number of geographic regions. Cadre members meet regularly with Wiggins and McTighe to review and share training techniques and strategies; critique drafts of new UbD-related publications; make recommendations for future directions of the framework; and identify exemplary educators, schools, and districts working with Understanding by Design.

This text presents a synthesis of the experiences and recommendations of study participants: educators who have used the UbD model for several years in various settings. Using data gathered from participant questionnaires, interviews, and focus groups, the book explores what high-level users suggest about the following:

• The design principles and strategies explicit in the UbD framework that have the greatest potential as points of leverage in promoting student achievement, staff performance, and organizational productivity gains.

• The implications of long-term UbD use for evaluating and improving standards design, curriculum development, assessment and evaluation, instruction, professional development, and school improvement planning.

• The inevitable problems and pitfalls that accompany the process of organizational change and renewal in educational settings, plus suggestions for addressing them.

• Recommendations to help schools and districts using Understanding by Design extend its application beyond the development of instructional units and into virtually all aspects of the learning organization.

The power of this book, we believe, lies in both the profound experiences of the individuals interviewed and the scope of their backgrounds. They truly represent a microcosm of the education profession. You will hear from teachers successfully implementing UbD in their classrooms, administrators collaborating with their staffs to implement UbD as part of their school improvement planning efforts, district-level leaders such as associate superintendents and supervisors, UbD cadre members, and college and university professors with extensive experience in cross-institutional partnerships involving UbD as a tool for preservice and teacher-induction programs.

Overall, the book is intended to help you assess two major levels of development within your learning organization: (1) strategies, processes, and recommendations for using UbD as a catalyst for school and district renewal and transformation and (2) "big ideas" and "enduring understandings" that can be first abstracted from the experiences of "high-level users" of Understanding by Design and then applied universally to the process of continuous improvement in learning organizations.

Education today is a complex and challenging arena undergoing profound transition and transformation. We hope that this investigation of Understanding by Design will contribute significantly to your individual and collaborative efforts to sustain and enhance the learning organization with which you are affiliated. We also hope that this book stands as a tribute to the brilliant contributions being made to education by the authors of UbD, Grant Wiggins and Jay McTighe.

John L. Brown
Understanding by Design Cadre Member

Introduction

■　■　■

ESSENTIAL QUESTIONS

1. How can Understanding by Design help educators address the accountability issues that they face in an age of rising expectations and diminishing resources?

2. What lessons have we learned from long-term users of Understanding by Design?

3. Beyond unit development, how can Understanding by Design improve the culture and effectiveness of learning organizations?

For many educators, the new millennium is a time of rising expectations and diminishing resources. We live in an age of high-stakes accountability, when the demand for tangible confirmation of the value of educational innovations is growing, sometimes to a deafening roar. Federal and state governments are experiencing the simultaneous aftershocks of increasing budget deficits and expanding demand for scientific confirmation of the value of specific educational programs and practices. If we are to retain and institutionalize educational initiatives, we must prove their effectiveness.

This book explores one such powerful educational innovation—Understanding by Design (UbD)—and what we know about its implementation, effects, and possible future application. The teachers,

1

administrators, national trainers, and college and university professors whose voices and experiences are captured here are all high-level users of UbD who have worked closely with its implementation process for several years. They were identified as successful practitioners by Grant Wiggins, Jay McTighe, and other members of the UbD training cadre, and they offered their feedback on the framework through a series of questionnaires. One-on-one interviews and focus groups reinforced initial data patterns and conclusions. These high-level users' analyses and insights represent the beginning of a long-term evaluation process of UbD, as well as a confirmation of its effect on the performance of students, staffs, and organizations.

The experiences of these high-level users, captured through their participation in this study, provide two intriguing and powerful lenses through which to examine this educational design framework. First, what we have learned about teaching for understanding reinforces how best to prepare all students for success in high-stakes accountability testing. Second, although UbD has so far emphasized unit development, high-level users universally affirm UbD's ability to improve the performance of schools in general. They hold that beyond its original purpose as an instructional design tool, UbD can be a powerful catalyst for organizational change, school reform, strategic planning, and continuous improvement.

This book offers a practical summary of insights and advice from high-level users to help you make the most of the UbD framework throughout your learning organization. It is especially useful for two primary audiences: (1) educators who are already working with UbD but need support in expanding and sustaining their efforts to improve student, teacher, and organization achievement and (2) individuals and groups who are new to UbD but can benefit from the lessons learned by such experienced users. Overall, this book provides a running commentary on lessons learned from the first five years of UbD's implementation. It synthesizes emergent themes, issues, and recommendations related to the following core issues:

- Initial training experiences and recommendations, including models and highlights of exemplary professional development programs related to UbD.

- Follow-up implementation strategies, emphasizing techniques for developing a UbD "community of learning."

- Implications of the curriculum design and development framework, including samples of systemic initiatives for curriculum reform that will incorporate UbD.

- Possible assessment and evaluation processes, such as using UbD to address and promote student achievement related to district and state standards and high-stakes accountability testing.

- Instructional strategies that promote student understanding, including lessons learned from differentiated instruction for special populations (gifted and talented, special education, English as a second language [ESL], and the socioeconomically disadvantaged).

- An exploration of UbD as a catalyst for team building, strategic planning, and organization development.

- Implications for preservice education, including UbD's use in colleges and universities, as well as in teacher-induction programs.

- Ideas about UbD's future, including high-level users' recommendations for modifications, additions, and enhancements.

In addition to the essential questions at the start of each chapter, this book's exploration of UbD revolves around the following questions:

1. Why should schools and districts consider adopting the goals and design principles of the UbD framework?

2. How have successful practitioners learned to use UbD to improve student achievement, curriculum, instruction, assessment, staff development, and organizational change?

3. How have those practitioners addressed the inevitable problems and issues associated with the change process and UbD?

4. How can we use UbD principles to build active learning communities?

5. What are the most practical and useful recommendations from successful high-level users for educators who are beginning to work with UbD, including strategies for all phases of implementation?

The following provides a quick overview of chapter content.

Chapter 1, "Implementing Understanding by Design: A Summary of Lessons Learned," provides an overview of the history and design elements of the UbD framework. For new or novice users, this chapter synthesizes key design principles and strategies, as well as UbD's research base. For both new and experienced users, Chapter 1 provides a comprehensive summary of lessons learned, issues cited, and recommendations made by a majority of the experienced UbD practitioners who participated in the study. It explores the recurrent ideas and essential questions posed by high-level users and investigates emergent recommendations, many of which are presented in the practitioners' own words. The chapter closes with the first of the book's nine organizational assessment questionnaires, which are suitable for use as part of school improvement and strategic planning efforts.

Chapter 2, "Designing and Developing School and District Curricula," explores how schools and districts are integrating the UbD framework into curriculum design, development, and implementation. This chapter provides practical advice about maintaining the traditional UbD unit focus while expanding its influence to address all areas of curriculum management. Chapter 2 concludes with a toolkit of proposed guidelines for curriculum developers to use when auditing and revising their curricula, using UbD principles and strategies.

Chapter 3, "Promoting Student Achievement and Addressing State and District Standards," confronts universal issues in educational assessment and accountability. How, for example, can UbD be used to improve student performance on standardized tests and related assessments? How can school staff members use UbD's principles and strategies to help all students succeed, especially those associated with special populations, such as gifted and talented, special education, ESL, and the socioeconomically disadvantaged? Perhaps most significantly, this chapter synthesizes high-level users' reflections on differentiated instruction and how UbD contributes to monitoring and adjusting instruction to accommodate the strengths and needs of individual students.

Chapter 4, "Promoting Student Understanding," examines the instructional implications of the UbD framework, emphasizing how successful practitioners have internalized the strategies and processes implicit in Stage Three's WHERETO template (see Chapter 1, page 19). Using the feedback and examples from successful teachers, administrators, and staff developers, this chapter describes how UbD principles can transform classrooms. The chapter provides useful recommendations related to differentiated instruction. How, for example, can we use a process of continuous improvement in our classrooms? How can we assess individual students' strengths and needs and address them throughout the implementation of standards-driven lessons, units, courses, and programs?

Chapter 5, "Promoting Exemplary Professional Development Programs and Practices," explores the relationship between the UbD framework and successful staff development programs and initiatives. This chapter emphasizes what high-level users have discovered about the best approaches to training and professional development related to successful Understanding by Design implementation. Beginning with a brief discussion of the special needs of the adult learner, the chapter summarizes training pitfalls and problems that result from failing to address participants' desire for meaningful and authentic experiences aligned with their expressed needs. Next, the chapter investigates how such ideas and processes align with contemporary change theory, including what is known about collaborative work cultures and the idea of continuous improvement as a guiding principle for successful professional development. It closes with a summary of how current electronic resources for Understanding by Design can complement district- and school-based professional development activities.

Chapter 6, "Improving Preservice Training and Teacher-Induction Programs," examines the critical issue of how we can best prepare teachers in preservice situations for success with all learners, particularly within the context of increasingly diverse student populations. Schools and districts face a double-edged sword: replacing growing numbers of retiring teachers while confronting demands for more rigorous accountability and higher student achievement in response to increasingly ambitious standards. This chapter addresses UbD's role in numerous preservice situations and venues, including college and university teacher-training programs and cross-institutional partnerships for professional development. Chapter 6 also describes successful teacher-induction programs in various school systems, with an emphasis on how sustained mentoring and professional development can support greater levels of new teacher retention and success.

Chapter 7, "Facilitating Organization Development, Continuous Improvement, and Strategic Planning," extends the investigation of UbD to the area of improving organizational cultures and the related process of strategic planning and continuous improvement. Every district has a protocol for school improvement planning. Frequently, however, this process is characterized by a top-down or committee-mandated plan that stakeholders too often disregard or misunderstand. Therefore, Chapter 7 examines what UbD implies for successful team building, collaborative work cultures, and institutional re-norming through organization development. It summarizes what experienced users suggest about forming a genuine learning organization that involves all stakeholders in the process of organizational reform and renewal.

The book concludes with Chapter 8, "Looking to the Future of Understanding by Design," which explores high-level users' views of the hot spots, trouble points, and future trends associated with education in the 21st century. This chapter investigates the relationship between UbD and emergent trends and themes, such as (1) federal and state testing and accountability initiatives designed to diminish the achievement gap and to ensure success for all; (2) the continuing need to improve focus areas such as curriculum, assessment, instruction, professional development, stakeholder involvement, and parent and community outreach; and (3) avenues for making connections and for forging links between the UbD framework and other national education renewal frameworks, such as Robert J. Marzano's What Works in Schools and differentiated instruction, as articulated by Carol Ann Tomlinson in *The Differentiated Classroom: Responding to the Needs of All Learners* (1999). The book ends with a series of vision statements as high-level users discuss the future of UbD in light of their experiences and insights.

■　■　■

Before you begin your journey through this book, consider two resources. Figure 0.1 summarizes the big ideas cited most frequently by high-level users who participated in the study. It reinforces the universal themes behind the UbD framework, plus the common pitfalls and limitations of the framework that most high-level users have experienced. Figure 0.2 translates those big ideas into the essential questions that experienced practitioners suggest are at the heart of their use of the UbD framework. Ideally, the ideas and questions will help to frame your exploration and understanding of Understanding by Design and help you make the most of the framework within your learning organization.

0.1 THE BIG IDEAS ABOUT UNDERSTANDING BY DESIGN MOST OFTEN CITED

1. Understanding by Design (UbD) is both a framework of research-based best practices and a language for unifying educators' work to promote high levels of achievement and understanding among students. It should not be presented to staff as "one more program to do" because most staff members already feel overloaded with accountability programs and related initiatives.

2. A primary value of UbD is its ability to get educators to identify the core ideas and questions that form the infrastructure of the content or disciplines that they teach. In effect, UbD promotes conversation about what is essential to the curriculum.

3. This focus on underlying concepts and questions provides a tool that educators can use to address the issue of time constraints. By building consensus about what is nonnegotiable for all students to know, do, and understand, they can identify an elegant curriculum that promotes all students' understanding and still ensure time for in-depth inquiry, questioning, and conceptual exploration.

4. UbD requires that its users genuinely know and understand the content for which they are designing a curriculum. For many users, UbD has led to professional dialogue and insight about the purposefulness and universal implications of subjects and programs.

5. The backward design process provides a set of principles that reinforce educators' analysis of accountability standards. By beginning with the end in mind, educators work collaboratively to determine what students should know, be able to do, and understand as students master content and reach performance standards.

6. In these times of high-stakes accountability testing, UbD provides a powerful rationale for expanding assessment repertoires to include performance-based assessments and students' reflections. UbD tools and processes support a "photo album" approach to monitoring student progress, rather than "snapshot" assessment measures based on tests alone.

Continued

7. UbD reinforces educators' ability to integrate assessment and instruction, thus leading to genuine differentiation that accommodates the unique strengths and needs of each student. Ideally, Stages Two and Three should be seamless in that teachers should constantly monitor student achievement as they modify instructional and learning behaviors that address a student's evolving strengths and needs.

8. Practitioners seek quantitative data to confirm UbD's value. Longitudinal evaluation studies to determine the effect of UbD implementation on student achievement, staff performance, and organizational productivity must be a major future priority.

9. UbD can and should expand beyond unit development. The next logical phase is for multiple districts to explore UbD's implications for and use in broader systemic curriculum design, development, and implementation. Until participants' unit designs are showcased in context within a district's curriculum, they remain stand-alone products, removed from an organizational context.

10. To this point, several key aspects of UbD have been either ignored or underemphasized and, thus, merit increased attention:

   • The need to create a national database synthesizing student achievement data in schools and districts with high levels of UbD use. Such a database can form the basis for a series of program evaluation studies that will determine the framework's effect.

   • The need to do much more with the connection between UbD and special populations, including gifted and talented, special education, ESL, and the socioeconomically disadvantaged.

   • The need to articulate a relationship between UbD and other widely disseminated initiatives for professional development and school improvement. Those initiatives include differentiated instruction, as articulated in Tomlinson (1999); What Works in Schools, as articulated in Marzano (2003); continuous

0.1 | **THE BIG IDEAS ABOUT UNDERSTANDING BY DESIGN MOST OFTEN CITED**

improvement and strategic planning; and performance assessment.

- The need to reconcile the connection between UbD and high-stakes accountability testing, including helping educators to overcome misconceptions about test preparation.

- The need to increase administrators' involvement in UbD, through means such as showcasing schools and districts that have made strides in making UbD a part of their organizational culture and instructional leadership. Additional models and exemplars aligned with best practices in continuous improvement are needed.

- The need to move forward in the use of electronic technology to create a national and international learning community regarding UbD. Currently, educators struggle to access and integrate the evolving structure and resources available through the UbD Exchange. In addition, there needs to be a more integrated, holistic approach to publicizing the use of UbD-focused videotapes, UbD-focused online courses, and Exchange-based exemplary units.

- The need for sustained, long-term collaborative inquiry into UbD, rather than one-shot training sessions.

- The need to build more cross-institutional partnerships among colleges, universities, and school districts that are responsible for integrating UbD into preservice teacher preparation and professional development programs. Although a growing number of preservice training institutions are using the framework, the perception lingers that UbD should be reserved for more senior staff members.

0.2 | THE ESSENTIAL QUESTIONS ABOUT UNDERSTANDING BY DESIGN MOST OFTEN ASKED

1. How do we overcome educators' anxiety and tension associated with the changes in mind-sets and practices required by UbD?

2. How can we expand our ability to access models, benchmarks, and exemplars of UbD units and related curriculum products?

3. How can we move beyond the initial training phase of UbD's implementation so we make UbD a natural part of our organizational culture and operating practices?

4. How can we overcome the misconception that UbD is just for the best and the brightest, and not for all students and staff?

5. How can we use our UbD experiences to transform staff attitudes and perceptions about standardized testing and overcome archaic notions of drill-and-kill teaching and test preparation?

6. How can we acquire and ensure the long-term availability of resources required to sustain successful UbD implementation (e.g., time, materials, curriculum development)?

7. How can we integrate UbD into our continuous improvement and strategic planning efforts?

8. How can we help teachers move beyond unit design and into unit implementation as they use the principles and strategies associated with each stage of UbD's backward design?

9. How do we make UbD a full staff effort, with instructional leadership by administrators and teacher-leaders who model and own this framework?

10. How can we ensure that UbD is a clear and natural part of instruction and learning for all students, including those in primary grades, those enrolled in special education or ESL instruction, and those who are socioeconomically disadvantaged?

IMPLEMENTING UNDERSTANDING BY DESIGN: A SUMMARY OF LESSONS LEARNED

ESSENTIAL QUESTIONS

1. *How does Understanding by Design provide a framework and a language to help educators promote all students' understanding?*

2. *How has Understanding by Design evolved since its initial publication? What are the major changes and trends associated with its evolution?*

3. *To what extent can educators abstract lessons learned about successful implementation of Understanding by Design and then apply those lessons to the process of strategic planning and continuous improvement?*

Understanding by Design (UbD) provides a common language for educators who are interested in promoting student understanding rather than formulaic knowledge or recall learning. It also provides a framework and a toolkit of research-based best practices that have been proven effective in helping educators to promote understanding-based results for learning, expand the range of assessment tools and processes they use to monitor student achievement, and enhance their design of instructional activities to promote high levels of student achievement.

This chapter summarizes the major lessons learned from successful UbD implementation as reflected in the experiences of educators who have used the framework for two or more years. The high-level users who participated in the study completed an online questionnaire (see Figure 1.1 at the end of this chapter), sat for one-on-one interviews, and took part in focus groups. The study asked them to respond to questions about UbD's effect on eight key areas:

1. Curriculum design, development, and implementation.

2. Assessment and evaluation of student performance.

3. Teaching for understanding, such as using differentiated instruction to address the needs of all learners.

4. Exemplary practices in professional development, including how UbD principles relate to the needs of the adult learner.

5. Organization development, strategic planning, and the continuous improvement process.

6. Cross-institutional partnerships related to all facets of new teacher induction and professional development.

7. The UbD "electronic learning community," including participants' reactions to resources such as the UbD Exchange, the ASCD UbD videotape series, and the relatively new area of Professional Development Online courses.

8. Our shared vision for education in the new millennium as an extension of experiences with UbD.

Understanding by Design at a Glance: A Brief History and Summary of Key Design Principles

Understanding by Design is the brainchild of Grant Wiggins and Jay McTighe, two internationally recognized experts in the field of curriculum, assessment, and teaching for understanding. Wiggins has a long and rich history of promoting the understanding of all students, particularly within the context of a backward design model. In addition to his award-winning publications on standards, assessment, and curriculum renewal, Wiggins is well known for his work with essential questions and curriculum auditing as part of his tenure with the Coalition of Essential Schools in partnership with Theodore Sizer.

McTighe received national recognition for his work with Robert J. Marzano and Debra Pickering in their ASCD publication *Assessing Student Performance Using Dimensions of Learning* (1991). The success of that publication reinforced McTighe's emergent leadership position within the movement to reform assessment practices in U.S. education.

Wiggins and McTighe had worked together extensively in both national and international venues, as well as during McTighe's tenure as the director of the Maryland Assessment Consortium. Their shared vision for a framework that could synthesize the best of what we know about promoting high levels of achievement for all students crystallized in their 1998 publication *Understanding by Design*. That book was followed by a series of supporting resources, including *The Understanding by Design Handbook* (McTighe & Wiggins, 1999) and *The Understanding by Design Professional Workbook* (McTighe & Wiggins, 2004); a comprehensive set of videotape resources and training materials; and the UbD Exchange, an international electronic database used as a compendium of UbD principles, strategies, and practitioner-generated unit designs.

Wiggins and McTighe underscore that Understanding by Design is a framework, not an educational program. In it, they have attempted to synthesize the best practices and the research-driven design principles associated with teaching and assessing for understanding. Although complex and challenging, their work speaks to educators who know, either from experience or from intuition, that discrete, atomistic instruction focused on traditional drill-and-kill approaches is guaranteed to produce little, if any, genuine learning or deep conceptual understanding among their students. Educators who have worked extensively with the Wiggins and McTighe framework almost universally acknowledge its commonsense recommendations for (1) unpacking curriculum standards; (2) emphasizing students' understanding, not just formulaic recall; (3) expanding assessment tools and repertoires to create a photo album of student achievement instead of a snapshot; and (4) incorporating the best of what current research tells us about teaching for understanding (including differentiated instruction) to meet the needs of all learners.

As we explore what high-level users and seasoned practitioners tell us about their experiences with UbD, we must keep in mind 10 major design principles at the heart of the Wiggins and McTighe framework:

1. Research tells us that students learn actively, not passively. Educators should consider the following big ideas when designing and delivering instruction:

   a. Students learn best when they actively construct meaning through experience-based learning activities.

   b. A student's culture, experiences, and previous knowledge (i.e., cognitive schema) shape all new learning.

   c. Learning depends on three dominant brain functions: (1) an innate search for meaning and purpose when learning; (2) an ongoing connection between emotion and cognition, including a tendency to slip into lower brain functions and structures when threatened; and (3) an innate predisposition to find patterns in the learning environment, beginning with wholes rather than parts.

   d. Learning is heavily situated; students' application and transfer of learning to new situations and contexts does not occur automatically. Teachers must help students to scaffold knowledge and skills; they plan for transfer by helping the learner move from modeling to guided practice to independent application.

e. Knowing or being able to do something does not guarantee that the learner understands it.

f. Students learn best when studying a curriculum that replaces simple coverage with an in-depth inquiry and with independent application experiences.

g. Students benefit from a curriculum that cues them into big ideas, enduring understandings, and essential questions.

2. Teaching for deep understanding emphasizes students' capacity for meaningful independent use of essential declarative knowledge (facts, concepts, generalizations, rules, principles, and laws) and procedural knowledge (skills, procedures, and processes). Students demonstrate genuine understanding when they express their learning through one or more of the following facets of understanding:

a. *Explanation:* The ability to demonstrate, derive, describe, design, justify, or prove something using evidence.

b. *Interpretation:* The creation of something new from learned knowledge, including the ability to critique, create analogies and metaphors, draw inferences, construct meaning, translate, predict, and hypothesize.

c. *Application:* The ability to use learned knowledge in new, unique, or unpredictable situations and contexts, including the ability to build, create, invent, perform, produce, solve, and test.

d. *Perspective:* The ability to analyze and draw conclusions about contrasting viewpoints concerning the same event, topic, or situation.

e. *Empathy:* The capacity to walk in another's shoes, including participating in role-play, describing another's emotions, and analyzing and justifying someone else's reactions.

f. *Self-Knowledge:* The ability to self-examine, self-reflect, self-evaluate, and express reflective insight, particularly the capacity for monitoring and modifying one's own comprehension of information and events.

3. At the heart of teaching for understanding is the creation of a consensus-driven curriculum that clearly distinguishes between and among what is just worth being familiar with versus what all students should know, be able to do, and understand.

4. The best instructional designs are backward; that is, they begin with desired results, rather than with instructional activities. UbD's backward design process involves three interrelated stages:

a. *Stage One:* Identifying desired results (such as enduring understandings, essential questions, and enabling knowledge objectives).

b. *Stage Two:* Determining acceptable evidence to assess and to evaluate student achievement of desired results.

c. *Stage Three:* Designing learning activities to promote all students' mastery of desired results and their subsequent success on identified assessment tasks.

5. Students develop deep conceptual understanding when they can cue into the enduring understandings and essential questions at the heart of their curriculum. Enduring understandings are statements that clearly articulate big ideas that have lasting value beyond the classroom and that students can revisit throughout their lives. Essential questions are big, open-ended interpretive questions that have no one obvious right answer. They raise other important questions, recur naturally, and go to the heart of a discipline or content area's philosophical and conceptual foundations.

6. Objectives that enable knowledge clearly specify, in measurable terms, what all students should know and be able to do to achieve

desired understanding and to respond to essential questions (Stage One). Ideally, understanding-driven objectives should begin with behavioral verbs reflective of one or more of the six facets of understanding: *explanation, interpretation, application, perspective, empathy,* and *self-knowledge* (Wiggins & McTighe, 1998, p. 44).

7. When designing Stage Two assessments of student performance, educators must keep in mind the metaphor of a photo album, rather than the more traditional metaphor of a snapshot. Effective monitoring of a student's progress should incorporate many assessment tools and processes, including these:

  a. Tests and quizzes with constructed-response (performance-based) items, rather than exclusive use of selected-response items (true-false, fill-in-the-blank, multiple choice).

  b. Reflective assessments, such as journals, logs, listen-think-pair-share activities, interviews, self-evaluation activities, and peer response groups.

  c. Academic prompts that clearly specify performance task elements, such as format, audience, topic, and purpose.

  d. Culminating assessment projects that allow for student choice and independent application.

8. A primary goal of teaching for understanding should be the assurance that students can use their acquired understandings and knowledge independently in real-world situations and scenarios. Culminating performance-based projects (what Wiggins and McTighe refer to as GRASPS), therefore, should include the following core elements:

G = *Goals* from the real world.

R = *Roles* that are authentic and based in reality.

A = *Audiences* to whom students will present final products and performances.

S = *Situations* involving a real-world conflict to be resolved, decision to be made, investigation to be completed, or invention to be created.

P = *Products* and *performances* culminating from the study.

S = *Standards* for evaluating project-based products and performances.

9. Teaching for understanding should involve activities that support identified desired results and integrate planned assessments (Stage Three). Wiggins and McTighe identify seven core design principles for teaching in an understanding-based classroom in a template they call WHERETO. Each of the letters in this acronym corresponds to key instructional design questions educators should always consider when planning learning activities:

W = How will you help your students to know *where* they are headed, *why* they are going there, and *what ways* they will be evaluated along the way?

H = How will you *hook* and engage students' interest and enthusiasm through thought-provoking experiences at the beginning of each instructional episode?

E = What *experiences* will you provide to help students make their understandings real and to *equip* all learners for success throughout your unit or course?

R = How will you cause students to *reflect, revisit, revise,* and *rethink*?

E = How will students *express* their understandings and engage in meaningful self-*evaluation*?

T = How will you *tailor* (differentiate) your instruction to address the unique strengths and needs of every learner?

O = How will you *organize* learning experiences so that students move from teacher-guided and concrete activities to independent applications that emphasize growing conceptual understandings?

10. Understanding by Design is not a program to be implemented; rather, it represents a synthesis of research-based best practices that are associated with improving student achievement. Successful UbD learning organizations are collaborative communities that emphasize practitioner inquiry, including the following:

a. *Peer Coaching:* Professional colleagues support one another by scripting lessons, providing focused feedback, and engaging in cognitive coaching (i.e., shared inquiry designed to align staff members' perceptions and judgments).

b. *Study Groups:* Colleagues study a text or explore an issue together and pool their experiences, reflections, and resources for understanding.

c. *Inquiry Teams:* Colleagues focus their study on a shared student achievement issue or an organizational problem that they wish to investigate together as an extension of their initial study group discussions.

d. *Action Research Cohorts:* Colleagues identify a research problem, hypothesis, or inquiry question concerning their learning organization; collect, analyze, and present available data; develop and implement an action plan related to identified solutions and interventions; and revise and modify their plan to reinforce a commitment to continuous improvement.

Voices from the Field: What Do Experienced Users Say About the Strengths and Challenges of Understanding by Design?

In light of these 10 major design principles, what do the teachers, administrators, trainers, and college and university representatives tell us about UbD's status and about their success making these principles come alive in their respective schools, districts, and related organizations? This question guides our exploration throughout this book. Let's begin by examining three major sets of conclusions related to study participants' perceptions about UbD's strengths, its challenges and potential pitfalls, and its potential future both in individual learning organizations and in the field of education in general. A sample of participants' survey responses follows each summary conclusion.

UbD's Strengths

High-level UbD users identified the following as framework strengths:

- The commonsense nature of UbD's principles and strategies.

- Its potential power for overcoming a tendency in public education to teach to the test and to emphasize knowledge-recall learning.

- Its ability to provide a common, consensus-driven language related to research-based best practices in the areas of curriculum, assessment, instruction, and professional development.

- Its potential for guiding and informing the process of school renewal and educational reform.

- Its ability to guide and inform educators' efforts to unpack standards and to help all students develop a deep conceptual understanding of what they are studying.

Q. What do you consider to be the greatest strengths of Understanding by Design?

A. "UbD is a philosophy for teaching and learning. Once you 'get it,' it is very difficult to go back to creating disconnected activities or covering facts without a broader context. It helps provide a narrative for the content or skills, which allows teachers and students to place this information in a context that is both meaningful and transferable. It

has allowed me, as a supervisor, to have rich and critical conversations with my staff and [has] provide[d] an internal check for teachers to be self-reflective."
—Mark Wise, social studies supervisor, Grover Middle School, Princeton Junction, New Jersey

A. "UbD makes sense. It reflects what good teachers do and is supported both by research and classroom practice. The three stages of backward design present a coherent guide for unit or lesson planning that teachers have a comfort level with. It also causes teachers to reflect on 'why' as well as 'what' they're doing."
—Joseph Corriero, assistant superintendent for curriculum and instruction, Cranford, New Jersey

A. "It is practical and research based. The power of showing teachers how to write essential questions, alone, makes it an extremely valuable resource."
—David Malone, senior vice president, Quality Learning, Missouri City, Texas

A. "Teaching for understanding and the templates and different entry points to make it happen [are UbD's greatest strengths]. Many teachers see this as a way to reclaim the creativity that they used to enjoy before the days of drill-and-kill for the test became so popular."
—Judith Hilton, UbD cadre member and university professor, Greenwood Village, Colorado

A. "[UbD's major strengths are] the logic of the basic model, the focus that is put on assessment, and the requirement to be clear about what is essential."
—Ken O'Connor, UbD cadre member, Scarborough, Ontario, Canada

A. "All three strategies—the backward design process, design standards, [and] performance tasks—can help teachers self-assess and engage in peer review, which can ultimately improve instruction."
—Alyce Anderson, principal, Herbertsville Elementary School, Brick, New Jersey

A. "[UbD's] focus on enduring understandings [is its greatest strength]. In this time of expanding knowledge, we are challenged to provide instruction that produces long-term results. UbD is one key to this effort."
—Elaine (Irish) Hodges, director of special projects and accountability, San Diego County Office of Education, San Diego, California

Challenges and Problems

When asked to reflect on the challenges and problems they encountered in working with Understanding by Design, high-level users consistently identified the following themes and issues:

• The critical need for educators to have time to reflect on what the UbD framework suggests about modifying existing practices and to try out various aspects of the backward design process in their classrooms.

• The inevitable issues that emerge with any change initiative or variable in educational settings, particularly a change that can be as challenging and sometimes threatening as UbD. Cited were staff members' resistance, confusion, and ambivalence to a framework that requires them to think and operate at a deep conceptual level.

• The very real dichotomy that exists in many schools and districts related to high-stakes accountability testing, including educators' misperceptions about the need to cover the curriculum and touch on everything that might be on the test.

• The challenge of moving UbD implementation beyond initial adopters and cheerleaders to include staff members who may be resistant, who may be fence-sitters, or who are hostile to new and provocative ideas.

• The need to make UbD implementation a long-term initiative that involves all organizational stakeholders, particularly administrators, who must become genuine instructional leaders and must clearly articulate the alignment between and among UbD and other account-ability initiatives within their school or district.

• The need to collect, analyze, and disseminate achievement data related to high levels of UbD use, particularly in light of current federal imperatives for any educational initiative to have a solid, empirical, scientifically confirmed research base.

Q. What do you consider to be the greatest challenges presented by Understanding by Design?

A. "Time and facilitation. Our greatest challenges have occurred in areas that have been traditionally skills-oriented [such as reading in primary grades and math in secondary grades]."
—Joseph Corriero, assistant superintendent for curriculum and instruction, Cranford, New Jersey

A. "Everyone within the system needs to be trained for maximum effectiveness. It should not be offered as a workshop for teachers only."
—David Malone, senior vice president, Quality Learning, Missouri City, Texas

A. "Having limited time to train staffs for a complete understanding of the process. One- or two-day workshops without follow-up rarely are effective in improving or changing teachers' planning process. Every group always wants more time. I frequently feel overviews provide little time to check for understanding of the process or to respond to misunderstandings of questions about the three stages [of backward design]. Teachers need to complete a unit design and go through a peer review to have a basic understanding of what UbD is all about. This is impossible to do in a one- or two-day workshop."
—Janie Smith, UbD cadre member and former curriculum developer, Alexandria, Virginia

A. "Too many one-shot, inoculation trainings are being done where teachers are expected to walk out of one, two, or three days of training

with enough understanding of UbD to change their professional practice. On top of it, they are expected to make these changes without any follow-up or support and under the watchful eye of someone who is the unit police and who knows the same or less than the teachers do about UbD."
—Elizabeth Rossini, UbD cadre member, Fairfax, Virginia

A. "UbD lacks empirical data. It's also hard to get people to make the shift from teaching facts and covering the content—[people] who either are not very bright or have spent years doing the other strategies and calling it teaching."
—Judith Hilton, UbD cadre member and university professor, Greenwood Village, Colorado

A. "Not enough research-based data that show [UbD] improves student learning. People want to know that it improves student learning. They want to quantify it."
—Elizabeth Rossini, UbD cadre member, Fairfax, Virginia

A. "[The greatest challenge is] rethinking one's approach to curriculum design and moving from coverage to uncoverage."
—Ken O'Connor, UbD cadre member, Scarborough, Ontario, Canada

A. "The greatest challenges involve breaking through the mind-set of traditional education. In [the United States], textbook- or activity-driven lessons head nowhere. We need [to help] teachers to have the courage to select the most important work that students should do and refine the lessons over time to improve results."
—Joyce Tatum, UbD cadre member and museum liaison, Normal Park Museum Magnet School, Chattanooga, Tennessee

A. "The greatest strength is also the greatest challenge. Teachers will ask, 'Why are we spending all of this time in Stage One?' They need to understand how important Stage One is. It is not about activities or coverage. Teachers don't want to put in so much up-front design time."
—Angela Ryan, instructional facilitator, Hershey, Pennsylvania

A. "The design is very complex—not easily understood or applied. When something this complex is added to existing responsibilities, it takes a long time to digest the information and apply it appropriately."
—Kay Egan, senior coordinator for special and gifted education services, Norfolk Public Schools, Norfolk, Virginia

A. "It is relatively complex. People do not think in terms of big ideas. Therefore, the more sharing, models, and support, the better."
—Elaine (Irish) Hodges, director of special projects and accountability, San Diego County Office of Education, San Diego, California

A. "[There is] too much emphasis on unit design. The UbD framework can also structure curriculum and districtwide decision making."
—Alyce Anderson, principal, Herbertsville Elementary School, Brick, New Jersey

A. "Our greatest challenge is to continue the work of lesson study. After the next museum night, we are planning a critical friend protocol of looking at student work schoolwide to determine quality."
—Jill Levine, principal; Judy Solovey, curriculum facilitator; and Joyce Tatum, UbD cadre member and museum liaison, Normal Park Museum Magnet School, Chattanooga, Tennessee

A. "UbD work is difficult and requires constant revision, particularly for teachers who have to 'unlearn' their prior practice. It can be time consuming (especially up front), and if not done correctly, teachers may not see the immediate rewards and [may] revert to past practice."
—Mark Wise, social studies supervisor, Grover Middle School, Princeton Junction, New Jersey

Resources for the Future

Finally, participants were asked what a school or district must provide to ensure the success of UbD implementation as part of the future of a learning organization. They emphasized the following recurrent recommendations:

• Ensure that there is an articulated purpose for Understanding by Design within the context of district and school strategic planning, emphasizing to all staff members how the UbD framework aligns with and supports student achievement goals.

• Provide support structures to ensure continuity and sustained professional development, including in-house trainers and coaches as well as financial resources.

• Ensure active administrative support for UbD implementation, targeting instructional leaders at both the school and central office levels.

• Avoid one-shot approaches to professional development, ensuring meaningful follow-up in the form of study groups and action research activities.

• Commit to collecting and analyzing "value-added" data to evaluate the relationship between high levels of UbD implementation and student achievement results.

Q. What is needed to support UbD implementation (e.g., human resources, financial resources, materials and supplies, professional development, curriculum reform)?

A. "A clearly articulated vision of where UbD work fits into the district's overall philosophy is absolutely necessary in order for teachers to buy in. Otherwise, it becomes another fad that will pass. Staff must understand that [UbD] is not 'this year's initiative,' but central to the district's vision of effective teaching and learning. It's what good teaching looks like in this district. Also needed [is] time for professional development and [for] facilitators to do the initial training."
—Joseph Corriero, assistant superintendent for curriculum and instruction, Cranford, New Jersey

A. "Clients need data that provide 'proof.' [In the] No Child Left Behind [era, we need] research-based assurance that professional development strategies and frameworks work. This promotes implementation. I have often thought that it would be valuable to have some units, complete with student work, as a part of the training materials—that's why I take those that I see in various places from different content areas and levels. It's a great selling tool."
—Judith Hilton, UbD cadre member and university professor, Greenwood Village, Colorado

A. "[We need] teacher leaders who have in-house capacity to support colleagues, a steady stream of funding, administrative commitment to ongoing professional development in UbD, and the ability to develop short- and long-range plans. Curriculum reform has some [effect], but scheduling modifications have little. Schools rarely see UbD explicitly connected to other issues and training. Too frequently, it's looked at as the topic du jour or 'this too shall pass.' "
—Janie Smith, UbD cadre member, Alexandria, Virginia

A. "On-site UbD experts are needed. Copies of the print materials are necessary for the school's professional library. If the school can afford it, as many copies as possible should be available for team members, on-site experts, trainers, etc. For it to be a part of the professional development process, the UbD philosophy must be a part of everyone's vocabulary. This takes time, ongoing feedback, and ongoing accountability in order for implementation and change to occur."
—Angela Ryan, instructional facilitator, Hershey, Pennsylvania

A. "[We need] UbD coaches who can assist schools with implementation. Though some training has taken place to have a few coaches available [in our district], anyone who is willing to coach has to take this as an add-on responsibility. Coaching is an important feature with great potential. It is unfortunate that [UbD] has not been given a fair chance to succeed."

—Kay Egan, senior coordinator for special and gifted education services, Norfolk Public Schools, Norfolk, Virginia

A. "As an administrative team, we need to continue providing time and focus [in order] for teachers to accept continual improvement as a way of professional life. After each term, we ask teachers what we should continue doing [and] what we should stop doing. What should we do more often and what should we do less often? What did we do well and what do we need to improve? The answers to these questions will help define future work."

—Jill Levine, principal; Judy Solovey, curriculum facilitator; and Joyce Tatum, UbD cadre member and museum liaison, Normal Park Museum Magnet School, Chattanooga, Tennessee

A. "Sustained and consistent professional development is the necessary first step in implementing UbD. This should lead to curriculum reform as well as [to] new resources that will nourish the new direction the courses will be taking. This will require the district to financially support the program in terms of providing in-service days and curriculum money."

—Mark Wise, social studies supervisor, Grover Middle School, Princeton Junction, New Jersey

■   ■   ■

As you reflect on these high-level users' reactions to Understanding by Design and compare your experiences with theirs, you may also wish to use these end-of-chapter resources to enhance your understanding.

Figure 1.1 presents the questionnaire that all study participants responded to. Which of the questions would you be able to answer at this point in your UbD use? Which of the questions would present difficulty to most staff members with whom you are now working? Do the issues that the questions raise provide any insight into your own future direction with the UbD framework, and do these issues have implications for your strategic planning process?

Figure 1.2 presents a detailed synthesis of the major ideas that are the foundation for all subsequent chapters, including (1) profiles of high-level users, (2) criteria for successful professional development, (3) alignment between UbD and other school and district initiatives, (4) effect on curriculum and assessment practices, and (5) general comments about other issues related to UbD's use and implementation.

Like all chapters in this book, this one ends with an organizational assessment matrix that summarizes the chapter's key ideas (see Figure 1.3). Each of these matrices represents the inferences and conclusions that can be drawn from this study of UbD and applied universally to all schools and districts as learning organizations. Ideally, even as stand-alone resources, these matrices can help school improvement teams benefit from the insights, lessons, and experiences of individuals who have worked with Understanding by Design as part of a district reform effort.

1.1	**UNDERSTANDING BY DESIGN HIGH-LEVEL USER QUESTIONNAIRE**

Part One: Participant Information

Please provide the following information so that we can compile a profile of the various individuals and groups completing this questionnaire.

1. Name:
2. Title/Position Currently Held:
3. Number of Years in Your Current Position:
4. Work Address:
5. Work Phone:
6. E-mail Address:
7. Number of Years You Have Worked with Understanding by Design in Your Organization:

School _____   District _____   University _____   Other _____

Part Two: Open-Ended Participant Questions

Please respond to each of the following questions in as much detail as possible. We are especially interested in your perspectives as both an individual practitioner/user of Understanding by Design and as a member of a broader organizational or district setting.

1. Please describe how you learned about and were trained in Understanding by Design.

2. How has your organization, school, or district provided professional development in Understanding by Design?

3. In addition to direct training (e.g., presentations, workshops, courses), to what extent are you currently using study groups, inquiry teams, action research cohorts, and other collaborative approaches to support UbD implementation? Which staff development activities have proven most effective? Which have been least effective or problematic? What would you recommend to others who are beginning UbD staff development?

4. How has your school or district attempted to help staff understand the purpose and uses of Understanding by Design? For example, how have you connected it to other district initiatives, policies, practices, and school improvement planning?

Continued

1.1	**UNDERSTANDING BY DESIGN HIGH-LEVEL USER QUESTIONNAIRE**

5. How has Understanding by Design been integrated into the design, development, and implementation of your school and district curriculum?

6. How does Understanding by Design support your work with student achievement of district and state standards, especially as measured by state and local accountability testing programs? Is there evidence you can cite of correlations between UbD use and test score gains or other evidence of improvement (e.g., student work quality, surveys of student engagement)?

7. How have Understanding by Design's instructional principles and strategies been integrated into daily classroom practice in the school(s) or district with which you work? What evidence can you cite to support your conclusions?

8. How is Understanding by Design being used to support strategic planning, continuous improvement, and organizational change? What evidence can you cite to support your conclusions?

9. Is Understanding by Design integrated into your teacher-induction program? If it is, please provide specific examples.

10. Please describe your experiences with and reactions to

    • The Understanding by Design Exchange
    • ASCD Understanding by Design videotapes
    • ASCD Understanding by Design online courses

11. What is needed to support UbD implementation (e.g., human resources, financial resources, materials and supplies, professional development, curriculum reform)?

12. What do you consider to be the greatest strengths of Understanding by Design?

13. What do you consider to be the greatest challenges presented by Understanding by Design?

14. Are there additional recommendations and suggestions you would like to make about the future direction of Understanding by Design?

1.2	**WHAT HAVE WE LEARNED ABOUT UNDERSTANDING BY DESIGN? A SUMMARY OF PRELIMINARY ASCD SURVEY AND FOCUS GROUP RESULTS**

1. High-level UbD users tend to

   a. Use the UbD unit design regularly in their professional duties.

   b. Participate in a collaborative follow-up to their initial training (e.g., study groups, action research cohorts, and peer reviews).

   c. Be responsible for helping to synthesize the relationship between UbD and other school and district accountability initiatives.

   d. Articulate UbD as a framework to describe research-based best practices, rather than as a stand-alone program.

   e. Understand the connection between UbD's design principles and the universal best practices in their field.

2. Successful and sustained UbD professional development tends to

   a. Avoid one-shot training sessions with little, if any, follow-up.

   b. Emphasize the alignment between UbD and other school and district accountability initiatives, especially standards and accountability testing.

   c. Involve all appropriate system stakeholders, not just single groups or cohorts.

   d. Ultimately involve some form of professional collaboration (e.g., initial study groups, peer review, and action research).

   e. Lead practitioners to express the need for value-added evaluations.

3. To emphasize the alignment of UbD with other district initiatives, school and district staffs

   a. Avoid presenting UbD as another required program.

   b. Articulate the relationship between UbD and district standards.

   c. Analyze the content of high-stakes accountability testing designs to articulate areas on those tests in which UbD supports student achievement.

Continued

1.2	WHAT HAVE WE LEARNED ABOUT UNDERSTANDING BY DESIGN? A SUMMARY OF PRELIMINARY ASCD SURVEY AND FOCUS GROUP RESULTS

    d. Integrate enduring understandings and essential questions into district curriculum frameworks and standards documents.

    e. Describe underlying design principles of UbD and their connection to districtwide initiatives to ensure the success of all students such as literacy development, mathematical problem solving, and differentiated instruction.

4. In schools and districts, UbD has influenced the curriculum and assessment processes as high-level users

    a. Provide controlling principles for unifying the articulation and implementation of standards.

    b. Establish a technology (through the three-circle audit process) for developing a viable core curriculum.

    c. Suggest tools and methodologies for unifying curriculum design.

    d. Emphasize the need for a photo album of assessment results, including constructed-response test items, reflective assessments, academic prompts, culminating performances and projects, and holistic and analytic rubrics.

    e. Establish a coherent set of instructional design principles through WHERETO.

5. Additional recurrent conclusions and recommendations include:

    a. The next logical step in UbD evolution is the systematic evaluation of UbD's effect on student achievement and organizational productivity.

    b. Although the electronic learning community for UbD has an established infrastructure, its potential has not been realized because teachers lack familiarity and face access difficulties.

    c. UbD implementation typically begins with a cohort of early adopters; however, sustained implementation is successful only

Continued

when it is organically blended into other systemic professional development and accountability programs.

d. Systemic UbD implementation is a process of organization development. Implicit UbD norms include collegiality, commitment to excellence and understanding, sensitivity to equity issues, professional development that is collaborative and job-embedded, and awareness of the learner as the center of the learning process.

e. Recurrent problems associated with UbD implementation include

   – Staff misperceptions that it is a stand-alone program.

   – Staff members' lack of deep conceptual understanding of curriculum content (and its big ideas, generalizations, and paradigms).

   – Professional desire for quick fixes and initiatives that do not require staff tolerance of ambiguity or complexity.

   – Misperceptions about teaching to the test.

   – Erroneous assumptions that teaching for understanding is for the gifted and talented only.

   – Beliefs that not all children can achieve deep conceptual understanding.

   – Fears about relinquishing the locus of control to the learner, plus deeply entrenched desires for managing classrooms through lecture and teacher-dispensed information sources.

   – Failure to provide financial resources to sustain site-based and job-embedded professional development.

f. There is a need to articulate the alignment between No Child Left Behind legislation and UbD to help ward off a perceived backslide toward teach-to-the-test instruction that overlooks the need for students to understand the content (both declarative and procedural) on which they are being assessed.

1.3	**ORGANIZATIONAL PRACTICES THAT PROMOTE UNDERSTANDING FOR ALL**

To what extent do organizations' practices within your school or district reflect each of the following indicators?

INDICATOR	NOT EVIDENT	SOMEWHAT EVIDENT	EVIDENT	HIGHLY EVIDENT
1. We share a common philosophy of learning that emphasizes student understanding, not just knowledge–recall.	☐	☐	☐	☐
2. Our standards clearly identify what all students should know, be able to do, and understand.	☐	☐	☐	☐
3. Our curriculum cues teachers and students into the big ideas and essential questions of each content area.	☐	☐	☐	☐
4. Our curriculum's objectives emphasize students' ability to explain, apply, and interpret what they are learning, not just to repeat or memorize it.	☐	☐	☐	☐
5. We reinforce students' ability to analyze perspectives and express empathy wherever possible.	☐	☐	☐	☐

Continued

INDICATOR	NOT EVIDENT	SOMEWHAT EVIDENT	EVIDENT	HIGHLY EVIDENT
6. We encourage a photo album approach to assessment that emphasizes performance assessment and self-reflection as key elements.	☐	☐	☐	☐
7. Our instruction emphasizes active student engagement and experience with learners at the center of the learning process.	☐	☐	☐	☐
8. Our professional development emphasizes study groups, inquiry teams, and action research processes.	☐	☐	☐	☐
9. Our long-range planning emphasizes our commitment to ensure that all students develop a deep conceptual understanding of our curriculum.	☐	☐	☐	☐

2

DESIGNING AND
DEVELOPING SCHOOL
AND DISTRICT CURRICULA

ESSENTIAL QUESTIONS

1. *What does Understanding by Design suggest about school and district curricula that promote high levels of achievement for all students?*

2. *How can Understanding by Design provide a set of design principles for educators working with curriculum design, development, and implementation?*

3. *How can Understanding by Design be integrated into the curriculum auditing and renewal process?*

Although Understanding by Design (UbD), as first presented in Wiggins and McTighe's 1998 book, focuses primarily on unit development, many of the most successful school and district adoptions of the UbD framework have gone beyond teacher-designed units. Those exemplary schools and districts have begun to use the principles of UbD to restructure their overall system of curriculum management. In this chapter, school and district curriculum leaders, working closely with teachers and administrators trained in UbD, explain how they have used the UbD framework to expand staff understanding of curriculum as a management system to promote continuous improvement. They also describe the challenges and potential pitfalls of integrating the UbD framework into school and district curriculum work in an age of test-driven accountability.

This chapter also examines curriculum work from schools and districts throughout the United States, emphasizing the following: (1) descriptions of how schools and districts have used UbD to promote staff and student understanding of content and performance standards; (2) examples of how schools and districts have integrated enduring understandings and essential questions into their curriculum frameworks and guides; (3) a discussion of how UbD's three-circle audit process can help schools and districts identify core enabling knowledge (i.e., what all students should know and be able to do); and (4) an exploration of how schools and districts are using UbD to promote a seamless relationship among curriculum standards, assessment, and instruction in core content areas. The chapter concludes with an organizational assessment that curriculum specialists can use to support an audit and revision of their curriculum.

The ideas and recommendations from high-level users of UbD concerning the framework's relationship to curriculum design, development, and implementation center on these core issues:

• A growing awareness that curriculum is a system for managing learning, not just for collecting documents or road maps for instruction. As part of this effort, we need to ensure that all staff members, including administrators and teachers, understand and address the concept of continuous improvement.

• The need for schools and districts to build consensus among all stakeholders about what content standards actually mean. That is, staff members must agree about what all students are expected to know and be able to do, as well as what they should understand.

• The value of integrating enduring understandings and essential questions into curriculum publications, including standards documents and related scope and sequence frameworks.

• The profound need to make the curriculum time-appropriate and realistic, auditing it to ensure that staff members have adequate time to teach for deep conceptual understanding, not just for superficial coverage.

• The potential power of the curriculum to reflect and model a range of assessment tools—what Wiggins and McTighe (1998) refer to as a photo album approach to assessment and evaluation. This helps a learning organization overcome an institutional reliance on selected-response testing as an exclusive way to monitor student performance and to determine organizational effectiveness.

• The opportunity that a well-designed curriculum provides to reinforce instructional practices that promote high levels of understanding and overall achievement for all students, including those in special populations (gifted and talented, special education, ESL, and the socioeconomically disadvantaged).

Patty Isabel Cortez, an English language arts coach at Morris High School in the Bronx, New York City, describes the power of Understanding by Design as a curriculum design process:

> UbD has often been referred to as "backward planning." It really is so much more than that. We are used to thinking about what we want our students to achieve and where we want them to be. Most of our effective teachers are already "backward planners." What is different about UbD? A [UbD] unit involves three stages: identify the desired results, determine acceptable evidence, and plan learning experiences and instruction. Understandings are often referred to as the "big ideas." These big ideas, or understandings, are statements that are provocative and are worded so that students may engage in meaningful discussions.

Like Cortez, many other high-level users reinforce the significance of UbD as a catalyst for transforming the curriculum as a tool to engage student ownership of what they are learning and to enhance their conceptual insights into the content they are studying.

Curriculum as a System for Managing Learning

One of the most significant findings in this study of high-level users was their universal agreement that the UbD framework offers a model for curriculum design, development, and implementation. Those practitioners agree that UbD synthesizes principles and strategies for continuous improvement in a school or a district. In effect, educators can use UbD as a tool to build consensus about the meaning of school and district standards, the implications of those standards on student learning, the ways to monitor and evaluate all students' progress in mastering those standards, and the instructional interventions needed to promote maximum student achievement and organizational effectiveness.

David Malone, senior vice president of Quality Learning in Missouri City, Texas, stresses that "UbD is a catalyst for change that clearly, [according to] research, offers a solution for more effective instructional planning. It is extremely powerful when wrapped in a total solution for school reform."

Similarly, Joseph Corriero, an assistant superintendent for curriculum and instruction in Cranford, New Jersey, reaffirms the value of UbD as a catalyst for unifying staff members' work with all phases of the curriculum development process:

> We have created a curriculum design template that reflects UbD principles. Teachers involved in writing curriculum are provided with additional training in Understanding by Design work. Teachers work with an outside consultant to design units of study that combine UbD with problem-based learning strategies.

What, then, would a school or a district look like if it approached its curriculum work using UbD principles to promote continuous improvement? High-level users agree on the following universal elements:

- Professional development for all staff members in the process of a curriculum audit using the three-circle audit process presented by Wiggins and McTighe (1998) and the three stages of backward design.

- Consensus building about the meaning of school and district standards for content and the standards' implications for what all students should know, do, and understand.

- Creation of exemplary curriculum materials that are field-tested and have proven effective in promoting high levels of student understanding.

- Integration of a range of assessment tools to monitor all students' progress in mastering identified standards.

- Feedback and coaching for all instructional personnel concerning their use of instructional strategies to promote high levels of student understanding and overall achievement relative to school and district standards.

According to high-level users, the process of helping a school or a district use UbD as a catalyst for continuous improvement involves a major commitment to consensus building and professional development. For example, Carl Zon, a standards and assessment coach and educational consultant in Sunnyvale, California, asserts that "the UbD-related work is intended to provide a common design framework for collaborative work by district teachers and administrators."

Similarly, Lynne Meara, supervisor of instruction and gifted and talented coordinator for the Plumsted Township School District in New Egypt, New Jersey, emphasizes that commitment:

[A]ll members of the staff have been trained or will participate in ongoing UbD instruction. The process has also been added to our differentiated supervision model in developing action research opportunities to develop more units using the process or exploring improvement possibilities for existing ones.

The big idea of curriculum as a system for managing learning entails educators' commitment to transforming curriculum into an organic process for promoting learning for all students. High-level users of UbD suggest that this approach must include the following components:

• Staff members' recognition that a curriculum is not simply written documents, but a living, breathing system for managing student progress.

• Consensus-driven determination of what mandated content standards suggest about what all students should know, do, and understand, with accompanying performance standards that articulate what students should demonstrate in terms of proficiency and competence at key points in their education, which would be ideally organized by grading or reporting periods.

• Integration of big ideas (including enduring understandings and essential questions) into both the design of curriculum standards and the evaluation of students' growing understanding of those standards.

• School- and district-sanctioned support of and commitment to using a range of assessment tools that include, but are not limited to, school-, district-, or state-mandated accountability tests (including constructed-response tests and quizzes; academic prompts that clearly specify format, audience, topic, and purpose; reflective assessment activities; and culminating performance-based projects).

• Learning environments that involve a continual connection between assessment and teaching, with the educator (1) monitoring all students' growing mastery of intended curricular outcomes and (2) modifying instruction to address individual strengths and needs.

- An overall school or district commitment to developing schools as learning organizations, with all stakeholders working together to promote maximum student understanding and achievement in relation to consensus-driven standards.

Building Consensus About Standards and Their Meaning

What, then, can we learn from high-level users about the issues relating to standards, and how can we best address those issues? Frank Champine, a social studies lead teacher (K–12) with the Neshaminy School District Department of Curriculum and Instruction in Langhorne, Pennsylvania, suggests that

> UbD represents a model for school reform at the most elemental level of a district. It gives teachers and administrators clear and simple guides on improving curriculum, instruction, and assessment. It enables teachers to analyze state and national standards in a meaningful way, and it gives individual teachers [or] practitioners an opportunity to control their professional lives.

All high-level users who participated in the study acknowledge that effective standards implementation has involved a process of consensus building and professional development. Angela Ryan, an instructional facilitator in Hershey, Pennsylvania, summarizes this process:

> The questions we ask during curriculum facilitation follow the UbD process. Whether we are designing standards/benchmarks/objectives, instructional strategies, or assessments, this is our process. It becomes our mantra.

Expert practitioners agree that a commitment to sustained professional discourse is essential to unpacking standards. Champine affirms that idea:

[UbD promotes] professional dialogue on critical elements of curriculum, instruction, and assessment. It forces teachers to share what is really important and how to teach it. The discussions that evolve from our training sessions are amazing. That dialogue brings people on board, and I see significant change in the instructional and assessment components of our teaching.

High-level users almost universally agree that work with school and district standards is both difficult and, at times, clouded by misunderstandings and misperceptions about the best ways to prepare students for high-stakes accountability testing. According to most interviewees, educators frequently misperceive test preparation efforts as a teach-to-the-test procedure; teachers directly coach students to be familiar with test design when "covering" content that may be on a particular state test. Understanding by Design, interviewees agree, reflects research-based best practices proven to help teachers transcend drill-and-kill approaches to test preparation with strategies that reflect five key principles:

1. Effective curriculum management systems require that curriculum standards be appropriate and reasonable for available time resources. Schools and districts can use the three-circle audit process (Wiggins & McTighe, 1998) to evaluate what is worth just being familiar with versus what is both essential and enduring.

2. Standards cannot be taught directly without consensus about their meanings. Educators must work together to determine what content standards suggest about what all students should know (i.e., core declarative knowledge, such as key facts, concepts, generalizations, rules, principles, and laws); should be able to do (i.e., core procedural knowledge, such as skills, procedures, and processes); and should understand at a particular point in their education.

3. Effective schools and districts integrate conceptual understanding directly into the design of curriculum frameworks. Most high-level users reinforce the need to have enduring understandings and essential

questions implied by school and district standards identified directly as part of core framework documents, including scope and sequence charts.

4. Curriculum documents must contain exemplars and benchmarks that model research-based best practices to promote student achievement and mastery of standards. This process should include assessments that reflect examples of accountability test design, as well as assessment prototypes that reflect a genuinely balanced approach to monitoring students' mastery of standards. Once again, practitioners acknowledge the value of Wiggins and McTighe's photo album approach, which replaces the limitations of assessment snapshots.

5. Instructional activities and design elements in effective curricula should reinforce staff members' use of research-based best practices. High-level users stress repeatedly the commonsense clarity of the WHERETO model for instructional design (see Chapter 1, page 19), which highlights instructional principles consistent with standards-based teaching and learning.

Integrating Big Ideas into the Curriculum Design Process

High-level users strongly agree about the need for schools and districts to overcome atomistic approaches to curriculum design. Students learn best when they can see the big picture in the content that they are studying, including recurrent themes, concepts, principles, and questions that need revisiting over the course of their education. When students are taught isolated or discrete pieces of information, high-level users concur, learning is minimized; in contrast, when students are taught using a conceptual approach that emphasizes understanding, levels of achievement for all students greatly increase.

The process of integrating big ideas into curriculum design emerges as a major aspect of practitioners' discussion of UbD and its effect on curriculum within their respective schools and districts. Deborah Jo Alberti, assistant director of special and gifted education services for the Norfolk Public Schools in Norfolk, Virginia, stresses that a major contribution of UbD has been that "the understandings and essential questions became part of the school division's curriculum guides." The Norfolk Public School District experimented with integrating enduring understandings and essential questions into all content areas assessed by the Virginia Standards of Learning accountability program.

Other school districts throughout the United States are approaching the integration of big ideas into their curriculum documents through a process of consensus building, coaching, and professional development. Dorothy C. Katauskas, assistant to the superintendent for curriculum, instruction, and staff development (K–12) in the New Hope–Solebury School District, New Hope, Pennsylvania, describes her system's approach as one that includes all key stakeholders:

> The most significant [effect of Understanding by Design] is probably the district's model for course outlines and curriculum maps. . . . We are mapping all curricula with the enduring understandings and essential questions as key component[s]. [Our] UbD Implementation Committee was inaugurated this year to study the change in culture as it relates to using UbD at the teacher, learner, and classroom environment level. That committee has Board [of Education] representation, as well as teachers and administrators.

High-level UbD users suggest that, in an ideal system of curriculum management, standards-driven understandings would be a fundamental part of curriculum design as follows:

• Enduring understandings (i.e., statements of understanding that articulate the big ideas and deep conceptual understandings at the heart of each content area) would be identified in all curriculum guides, with an emphasis on conceptual statements that students would revisit across grade levels.

• Essential questions (i.e., open-ended, interpretive questions that go to the heart of a discipline or content area) would give teachers and students cues about how to inquire into the essential meanings and understandings that form the infrastructure of the content that they are teaching and learning.

• Enabling knowledge objectives (i.e., objectives derived from content standards to articulate specifically what students at a particular grade or within a particular reporting period should know and be able to do) would emphasize student understanding through behavioral verbs aligned with one or more of the six facets of understanding (explanation, interpretation, application, perspective, empathy, and self-knowledge).

• Those big ideas would guide and inform assessment and instructional decision making and would cue both teachers and students into what is universal or essential about the curriculum that they are exploring together.

Judith Hilton, a UbD cadre member and university professor from Greenwood Village, Colorado, describes the benefits of this particular curriculum component:

> [As a result of Understanding by Design,] teachers more deliberately unpack the content standards and align the topic to the standards. I see teachers teach more to what students should learn than the fact [or] skill orientation. They are improving in developing a comprehensive assessment plan and looking at evidence of performance over time. It is interesting to see what happens as teachers struggle to shift the paradigm to teach conceptually. When they do that pretty well, the daily plans become a struggle, so I find it necessary to spend more time on Stage Three than I logically expect, [because] daily instruction is most teachers' strength. The big idea

sinks in when they get student work, particularly [work that is] better than they have [seen] in the past. That is when they fall in love with the idea.

Overcoming Time Constraints Through Curriculum Auditing

Educators everywhere decry the absence of realistic time resources in the face of mounting calls for accountability in their schools and districts. Therefore, it is no surprise that many high-level UbD users reinforce the need for educators to revisit their curriculum to ensure that it presents a realistic course of study within available time constraints. Many practitioners also testify to the value of the three-circle audit process described by Wiggins and McTighe at the beginning of *Understanding by Design* (1998). Specifically, the authors recommend that, as educators work together to unpack standards and implement required curricula, they ask themselves three key design questions:

1. For each of our required standards, what is worth just being familiar with? That is, what can we teach relatively superficially, or what can we eliminate from our instruction when we are confronted with time constraints?

2. If we examine each of our standards, what should all students know (i.e., core declarative knowledge) and be able to do (i.e., core procedural knowledge)?

3. In light of what we agree all students should know and be able to do, what are the implied enduring understandings and essential questions that they should explore and about which they should demonstrate growing proficiency and competence?

Ryan of Pennsylvania asserts that

[Understanding by Design] is a proven way to make sense of what one is teaching. It helps with the efficiency of time for instruction in the classroom. You take the students where you want to go . . . educationally. As a teacher, I become forced to design and [to] plan the deeper understandings. I recognized through UbD how to get students where I wanted them to go by design—and not by chance.

Linda Marion, a staff development resource teacher from Chula Vista, California, describes a similar process and benefit:

Having teachers stop and think about what the enduring understandings were (what did they want their students to remember and use years from now), [determine] acceptable evidence (valid and reliable) that the students [had] gained the understanding, and [sift and sort] through their repertoire of activities and lessons was quite a paradigm shift in and of itself. Teachers were thinking about what they were teaching. They were evaluating each and every assignment and assessment to ensure validity. Teachers were letting go of time-honored and favorite lessons and activities that were not aligned to the desired results. This was BIG, really BIG!

Interviewees confirm that true progress in promoting achievement for all students, including those identified as special populations, requires schools and districts to eliminate the "mile-wide, inch-deep" curriculum and to replace it with one that allows genuine teaching for understanding within a progress continuum. Educators must have the time and resources to promote understanding for all, not just for a select or highly able few.

Curriculum as a Platform for Research-Based Best Practices

I see UbD as a way of thinking about design. It is not a prescriptive program that gets put on a shelf. It becomes a series of questions that [educators] ask themselves when they think about design of curriculum [or] instruction at any level. I also see it as a powerful way to put the responsibility for learning back in the students' hands. It allows students to become active and not passive members of the

> learning community. And it gives teachers a way to become more of a facilitator and a coach. It helps teachers focus on their students and what is right for their students. I wish that I had worked this way when I was a classroom teacher.

This reflection from Elizabeth Rossini of Fairfax, Virginia, one of the UbD cadre members interviewed for this study, reinforces another highly consistent theme among high-level users: the need for a viable system of curriculum management that identifies, reinforces, and models the research-based best practices in all curriculum materials and related resources. As Elliott Seif, a UbD cadre member and a former curriculum and staff director in Bucks County, Pennsylvania, suggests, "The best model is when curriculum matches UbD principles, or [teachers] have worked with their supervisory model to integrate UbD indicators into instructional supervision."

Janie Smith, a UbD cadre member and former curriculum director in Alexandria, Virginia, affirms

> [Understanding by Design] works in effectively improving the planning process and focusing on desired results [through] the backward design approach. Many teachers don't plan using a unit approach, but focus on daily lessons and "coverage or activities." UbD proves less can be more when it comes to in-depth understandings, retention, and transfer of learning to new and varied situations. Performance assessment training is also a strength.

Katauskas of Pennsylvania emphasizes another recurrent theme in the study: the need for collaboration and consensus building in a systemwide process of effective curriculum management:

> [Our UbD Implementation] Committee is . . . developing a model similar to the well-known "Walk Through" model of school study, but it will solely focus on UbD as a data collection model from both the qualitative and quantitative point of view. These forums will be

opportunities for internal staff to review indicators of understanding that we are developing by interviewing teachers and students, as well as [by] viewing the classroom environment. Then the teams will discuss their observations with the teachers in a feedback model [using] the action research strategy. We would like to eventually open the forums to other UbD district visitors who would understand the indicators and provide external feedback also.

Expert practitioners underscore the value of UbD's WHERETO template (see Chapter 1, page 19) as a clear, accessible, and powerful synthesis of what we now know about the teaching and learning process. It is necessary, they suggest, to apply the WHERETO components to all aspects of curriculum design, development, and implementation. In particular, they agree that WHERETO reinforces such key principles as *continuous improvement* (i.e., using a sustained feedback-adjustment system to identify students' strengths and needs and design instruction to accommodate them); *differentiation* (i.e., personalizing the teaching-learning environment based on students' interests, goals, academic performance, and achievement gaps); and *academic rigor* (i.e., ensuring that all learners receive an understanding-based education reflecting the values of excellence and equity). At the same time, survey participants are concerned about the complexity and challenges of putting these principles and processes into action in light of the high-stakes accountability testing many public schools and districts now face. In fact, many participants decried the proliferation of misconceptions and misunderstandings about how to best promote high levels of performance on such tests (i.e., mechanical drill-and-kill test preparation focusing on discrete curriculum elements presented in isolation vs. conceptually-organized teaching and learning based on inquiry into the big ideas, concepts, and essential questions underlying content areas).

As you consider what this chapter has suggested about UbD and curriculum as a system for managing learning, you may wish to use the following end-of-chapter resources to guide staff exploration, particularly study group inquiry.

Figure 2.1 synthesizes the major themes and big ideas from this chapter as a tool for exploring curriculum reform. Figure 2.2 provides an organizational assessment matrix summarizing the universal design principles that can be abstracted from UbD and applied to evaluating any system of curriculum management. Once again, the power of the UbD framework is its universality and its ability to guide and to inform dialogue about educational renewal efforts, whether or not staff members have participated in formal training or unit development that covers Understanding by Design.

2.1   RECOMMENDED CURRICULUM DESIGN PRINCIPLES

1. Curriculum should be viewed as a system for managing student learning, not as a series of documents.

2. Curriculum must be elegant and realistic for time and resource constraints within the school and district. The three-circle audit process supports this approach by encouraging teachers to determine what is worth being familiar with (i.e., content that can be covered superficially or given abbreviated attention, if necessary), what all students should know and be able to do, and what all students should understand at a deep conceptual level.

3. State and district standards should form the basis for framing all major curriculum questions. Curriculum is the tool through which learning organizations unpack standards, a process that requires consensus building and interpretation. Educators may not immediately interpret or understand standards in the same way.

4. Effective curriculum requires that key framework documents (e.g., scope and sequence charts) articulate not only content standards (i.e., what all students should know and be able to do), but also big ideas, enduring understandings, and essential questions. Curriculum should be organized conceptually; universal elements should form the infrastructure for curriculum programs, subjects, courses, and units.

5. Conceptual organization of curriculum requires that designers and developers achieve consensus regarding horizontal elements (i.e., what should be taught within a particular time period); vertical elements (i.e., how various time periods and grades interrelate); and spiral elements (i.e., big ideas, essential questions, and enabling knowledge objectives that are to be revisited across time periods and content areas).

6. High-impact curriculum models show teachers how to address content standards, big ideas, and recurrent universal questions so that all students learn them at increasing levels of conceptual understanding.

Continued

7. To promote continuous improvement, curriculum must demonstrate how teachers can use a range of assessment tools (i.e., tests and quizzes with constructed-response items, reflective assessments, academic prompts, and culminating projects) to monitor student achievement and adjust instruction to accommodate emerging strengths or needs.

8. Curriculum guides should reflect research-based best practices that embody the following principles:

   • Ensure that all students know where they are going and why.

   • Incorporate warm-up activities that establish purpose, evince authenticity, and encourage student ownership.

   • Allow students to explore big ideas and essential questions.

   • Encourage students to be self-reflective and self-evaluative.

   • Reinforce students' capacity for self-monitoring, self-assessment, and self-presentation.

   • Use differentiated instruction to address all learners' needs.

   • Move students from concrete experience to deep conceptual understanding.

2.2 CURRICULUM DESIGN AND DEVELOPMENT PRINCIPLES THAT PROMOTE UNDERSTANDING FOR ALL

To what extent does curriculum in your school or district reflect each of the following indicators?

INDICATOR	NOT EVIDENT	SOMEWHAT EVIDENT	EVIDENT	HIGHLY EVIDENT
1. Our curriculum is clearly aligned with our approved content standards.	☐	☐	☐	☐
2. Our curriculum documents emphasize the big ideas and essential questions of key content areas.	☐	☐	☐	☐
3. Our curriculum objectives align with one or more of the six facets of understanding.	☐	☐	☐	☐
4. Our curriculum reinforces the need for teachers to use a range of assessment tools, including performance tasks, reflective assessments, and culminating projects.	☐	☐	☐	☐
5. Our curriculum reinforces the need for students to be clear about where they are headed and why they are going there.	☐	☐	☐	☐
6. Student engagement in the curriculum and a sense of ownership are content priorities.	☐	☐	☐	☐

Continued

INDICATOR	NOT EVIDENT	SOMEWHAT EVIDENT	EVIDENT	HIGHLY EVIDENT
7. Our curriculum emphasizes self-reflection and self-assessment.	☐	☐	☐	☐
8. Our curriculum emphasizes differentiated instruction to meet the needs of all students and to maximize their demonstration of evolving understanding.	☐	☐	☐	☐
9. Our curriculum is organized conceptually and moves students along a continuum from teacher-guided experience toward independent application, interpretation, and explanation.	☐	☐	☐	☐

3

PROMOTING STUDENT ACHIEVEMENT AND ADDRESSING STATE AND DISTRICT STANDARDS

ESSENTIAL QUESTIONS

1. *How can educators' use of the principles and strategies of Understanding by Design improve the achievement of all students?*

2. *What has been learned about the relationship between Understanding by Design and students' mastery of state and district standards?*

3. *How can educators' adoption of the principles and strategies of Understanding by Design enhance their approach to assessing and evaluating student progress?*

High-stakes accountability testing in the United States—highlighted recently by the passage of the federal No Child Left Behind legislation—has led to great concern and even consternation in districts with underperforming schools. Virtually all high-level users report grappling with standards and accountability issues in one way or another. They frequently express frustration at the misunderstood and problematic instructional practices associated with some test preparation efforts, and they agree that using UbD principles can support schools and districts in turning around underachieving and at-risk schools. In particular, practitioners make a variety of suggestions about how educators can monitor, assess, and evaluate student achievement in relationship to state and district standards. Perhaps most significantly, they reinforce the value of students taking an active role in the evaluation process through self-expression, self-regulation, and self-evaluation.

Successful high-level users emphasize UbD's strategies for ensuring that teachers begin with the end in mind, thereby addressing the important link among desired results (including enduring understandings and essential questions), assessment, and instruction. They also stress how UbD has improved teachers' use of formative and summative assessment processes, including the six facets of understanding, when monitoring and assessing student progress. Perhaps most important, these users reveal how they have improved their use of a range of formal and informal assessment tools, such as creating photo albums of student progress rather than snapshots and using performance tasks, reflective assessments, interviews, observations, tests and quizzes, and GRASPS culminating projects (see Chapter 1, page 18).

Addressing State Accountability Standards

Mark Wise, social studies supervisor for Grover Middle School in Princeton Junction, New Jersey, reflects on the challenge facing many educators in schools and districts that use Understanding by Design:

> We have been unable to gather data that would indicate that UbD has had an [effect] on student performance. We have only a handful of teachers who are practicing the UbD philosophy faithfully, and [although] we have statewide testing at the end of 8th grade, it is difficult to determine which teacher had the greatest [effect] on the students' performance. As well, we have yet to develop valid

and reliable performance assessments. However, UbD has been very helpful in mining the standards for important understandings so that we are using the standards, as well as other resources, to develop the most meaningful and sequentially and developmentally appropriate course of study.

Within the area of assessment and evaluation, educators face a striking paradox. Because the use of UbD at a systemwide level is at a relatively early stage, high-level users generally describe a lack of longitudinal evaluation data about UbD and its effect on standardized test scores. However, their own use of UbD consistently confirms their perceptions of the framework's close alignment with successful preparation of students to master state standards. For example, Jill Levine, Judy Solovey, and Joyce Tatum—principal, curriculum facilitator, and museum liason, respectively—of the Normal Park Museum Magnet School in Chattanooga, Tennessee, comment

> Our UbD units are aligned with the State of Tennessee Standards, and the knowledge and skills tested on the TCAP [Tennessee Comprehensive Achievement Program Tests]. By embedding knowledge and skills in understandings and performance assessments, [as] our case exhibits, we know that isolated facts have a purpose and a "stick-to-it-ness" not normally found in elementary classrooms. As part of the quarterly exhibit, students are routinely asked to write labels about [the] how, what, why, and so what of content and [to] apply the work to understanding-focused study. Each student is asked to have an electronic portfolio entry providing evidence of the level of understanding. At the end of this school year, teachers and parents will complete a survey of how effective we are, and the quality of student work will be addressed. Anecdotal evidence is positive.

What do high-level users cite as the strengths and contributions of UbD to school and district efforts to address state standards? Although reactions vary according to the length of time each respondent has used the model, the following conclusions emerge from the totality of interviews, focus groups, and questionnaire responses:

- Educators have improved the level of their discussion and dialogue concerning the nature of district and state standards and the implications of these standards for student learning.

- UbD unit development has forced high-level users to achieve consensus about what is essential for all students to know, do, and understand in each course and at each grade level.

- There is a heightened commitment to separating significant content elements from insignificant content elements, particularly the enduring understandings and essential questions implicit in curriculum standards.

- As a result of this attention to the curriculum's essential elements, versus what elements are worth just being familiar with, high-level users acknowledge increased attention to students' ability to explain, interpret, and apply at an independent level what they have learned.

- High-level users universally acknowledge the power of Stage Two in emphasizing the expansion of assessment repertoires, including a growing emphasis on students' self-reflection and self-regulation.

- The GRASPS performance task and project design template (see Chapter 1, page 18) has increased educators' attention to helping students move beyond teacher-guided instruction to real-world, authentic application of the knowledge, skills, and understandings implicit in district and state standards.

- According to high-level users, many Stage Three instructional design elements reinforce school- and district-level work with standards and student achievement through WHERETO (see Chapter 1, page 19).

Patty Isabel Cortez, an English language arts coach at Morris High School in the Bronx, New York City, summarizes the demands of balancing standards and teaching for understanding:

> The challenge as always is to merge these discussions—the assignments, understandings, [and so on]—with the very concrete demands of the [English language arts] and Math Regents. Thus, we forge ahead and attempt to apply as many effective instructional initiatives as is educationally possible. I consider UbD to be one of these effective approaches and hope to continue creating units for our colleagues and ultimately for our pupils.

Student Understanding and District Standards

Study participants' perceptions about connections between high levels of UbD use and staff understanding of district standards extend to the critical issue of how well students grasp what *they* are expected to know, do, and understand. Respondents provide anecdotal evidence of growth in student learning and mastery of standards, consistently citing increases in students' deep conceptual understanding, improvement in students' ability to apply what they have learned to the world beyond the classroom, and increases in students' capacity for self-regulation and self-evaluation using rubrics and scoring guides that reflect school and district standards.

Marnie Dratch, a 6th grade language arts teacher at Grover Middle School in Princeton Junction, New Jersey, summarizes her experience of students' enhanced performance:

> Backward design has greatly improved my teaching practice and student performance. Through careful consideration of the desired . . . result, I am able to identify the concepts that I want the students to understand at the completion of a unit. With this in mind, I can design my lessons based on those understandings. The lessons then correspond directly to the skills needed to achieve the desired results.

Like many high-level users, Dratch attributes improvement in her students' ownership of mandated standards to her stepped-up efforts to make Stage One's desired results the primary focus for her instructional design:

> Students see a more focused and organized unit and can clearly identify the purpose of each lesson. In addition, I now expose students to many samples of completed projects at the beginning of a unit so that they have a clear understanding of the intended goals.

Additionally, expert UbD practitioners confirm the power of the framework's emphasis on the learner as the center of the learning process. Once again, Dratch speaks for many high-level users:

> It helps when the students themselves identify the characteristics of an exemplary project so that they will have a clearer understanding of the parts of the whole. [For me,] as a language arts teacher, this means exposing students to many student-generated and professional writing samples, guiding students to identify exactly what makes each a strong (or weak) writing piece, identifying the necessary writing skills, and teaching those skills. Students now have a "map" for each unit, [which] seems to make them much more enthusiastic about the process. With clearly defined units, more purposeful lesson plans, and more enthusiastic students, UbD has made teaching a lot more fun!

At the conclusion of this chapter, Figure 3.1 presents a detailed summary of learner characteristics that are present in schools and classrooms using high-level UbD. Briefly, high-level users who note UbD's positive influence on student achievement (especially in relation to growing mastery of standards) tend to cite the following:

• Increased evidence of students' active engagement in the learning process.

• Enhanced sense of student efficacy as students express a growing understanding of what they are learning and why they are learning it.

• Expanded student awareness of the big ideas, enduring understandings, and essential questions that underlie the more discrete parts of the curriculum.

• Increased student involvement in all phases of the evaluation process, including self-monitoring and self-evaluation in relation to grade-level standards, course standards, unit standards, or all three.

• Increased evidence of students' capacity for self-expression and presentation of their learning in relation to such facets of understanding as explanation, interpretation, and application.

Cortez of New York City summarizes how her students have changed since she began implementing Understanding by Design:

> Since our district has adopted UbD as its instructional initiative, I've recommended that we all start to think about "big ideas [or enduring] understandings" as they complement [relate to] our units. One very significant advantage to planning units using the UbD format is that texts, activities, [our district] standards, and student outcomes have taken on a concrete quality. Classroom discussions tend to take on a more urgent and enthusiastic tone because students tend to be willing to explore issues that are very real to them in their own daily lives. These discussions are often more animated, opinion based, and loud!
>
> UbD has helped me to organize the details of literary texts according to their real-life, authentic value to a teenager's life. Students' products tend to be rooted in real-life problems with real-life applications. As in life, students' products never present definitive solutions; instead these assignments are "in the gray of life"—explorations. The task, guidelines, evaluation, and criteria, however, are very clear. These assignments encourage students to be creative thinkers [about] real-world scenarios.

Using a Range of Assessment Tools and Processes

The value of using multiple forms of assessment to monitor student progress and to modify instruction to promote understanding for all is a recurrent theme that high-level users associate with an effective assessment and evaluation process. At the Normal Park Museum Magnet School in Chattanooga, Tennessee, for example, Levine, Solovey, and Tatum assert the following:

> UbD has become a unifying force for curriculum development. All work starts with what we want students to understand, question, know, and be able to do. The performance assessment takes the form of an exhibit at the end of the term, and smaller exhibitions of understandings are evident throughout the unit.

> The greatest strength of UbD is [that it is] multifaceted. First, it provides a philosophical foundation for making instructional decisions at the building and grade level. The planning process causes teachers to examine practices and make sound decisions about what we want students to understand. The process sets priorities for what is important, sets learning in the real world of performance tasks, and, finally, decides what strategies and content [are] included to prepare students for the assessments as students self-assess their progress, understanding, and performance.

High-level users consistently acknowledge the value of the backward design in Stage Two, particularly the way in which it reinforces the need to use the following four interrelated assessment processes to monitor students' growing understanding and support their achievement:

1. *Tests and quizzes with constructed-response items*. Reinforce student understanding by incorporating performance-based assessment tasks and activities, particularly ones that reflect the design principles that students may encounter on high-stakes accountability tests. Wherever possible, align constructed-response assessment items with behaviors associated with one or more of the six facets of understanding.

2. *Reflective assessments.* Use tools such as reflective journals, think logs, listen-think-pair-share activities, and peer coaching and peer response groups to encourage students' self-monitoring, self-regulation, and self-knowledge. High-level users cite UbD's influence in promoting staff commitment to students' involvement in the evaluation process, as well as the considerable value of the metacognitive tools used in that process.

3. *Academic prompts.* Structure performance-based assignments so that students are clear about what is expected of them, including the format that they are to use, the audience for whom they are to design their performance, the specific topic(s) that they are to address, and the purpose(s) of the assignment.

4. *Culminating projects.* At least once during a grading or reporting period, assess students' capacity for independent use of what they are learning in reality-based scenarios, simulations, and other forms of independent project-based work. High-level users praise the clarity and practicality of UbD's GRASPS template (i.e., all projects should clearly describe student *goals, roles, audience, situations, products* and *performances*, and evaluation *standards*).

Addressing the Needs of Special Populations

Educators today are struggling with the issue of how to reconcile standards, standardized testing, and statewide accountability programs with the use of differentiated instruction to address the unique strengths and needs of the individual learner. Many high-level users decry educators' inadvertent misinterpretations of how best to prepare students for high-stakes testing. Virtually all high-level users emphasize that drill-and-kill test preparation efforts can impede genuine student understanding and detract from the time needed to promote deep conceptual understanding among all learners. They also emphasize that UbD's design principles represent a powerful synthesis for differentiating instruction to accommodate the needs of special populations, including students identified as gifted and talented, special education, ESL, or socioeconomically disadvantaged.

When high-level users discuss the needs of special populations and the ways in which UbD can address such needs, they generally stress the UbD framework's ability to accommodate differentiated instruction in a context of high expectations for all learners. Practitioners interpret the UbD framework as requiring a deep commitment to rigorous core standards that can be unpacked for student understanding—all students' understanding—through tools such as enduring understandings and essential questions. Additionally, the declarative (facts, concepts, generalizations, rules, laws, and principles) and the procedural (skills, procedures, and processes) knowledge that students are expected to master can be presented in higher-order objectives that are aligned with one or more of the six facets of understanding.

Most respondents express a deep respect for the ways in which UbD exhorts educators to have high expectations for all learners through desired results aligned with deep conceptual understanding, not just knowledge–recall learning. Respondents have also emphasized the value of the photo album approach for Stage Two's assessment design as a controlling idea for differentiated instruction for special populations. In effect, once educators establish a core curriculum with a rigorous set of desired results, they can use a range of assessment tools to monitor all students' growth in mastering those results. Gifted and talented specialists, such as Deborah Jo Alberti of the Norfolk Public Schools in Norfolk, Virginia, and Lynne Meara of the Plumsted Township School District in New Egypt, New Jersey, cite UbD's usefulness for creating a tiered curriculum and for compacting the curriculum. If teachers determine what students already know and understand at the beginning of units, they can move those who have already mastered core content to more accelerated and independent projects and explorations.

A differentiated instruction process involving multitiered assessments, ongoing monitoring, and adjustment of instruction to accommodate individual students' strengths and needs also complements the needs of students who may be struggling academically. Multiple assessment tools allow educators to capture a full range of student performance data, rather than the restricted snapshot of tests used in isolation. This process of individualized assessment and evaluation relative to Stage One's desired results also complements educators' work with diverse student populations, including students with language limitations. Many high-level users comment that Understanding by Design is at odds with a one-size-fits-all approach; it expands educators' ability to capture a full portrait of student progress.

Most respondents also state that Stage Three's instructional design template, WHERETO (see Chapter 1, page 19), contains many strategies and principles that support differentiated instruction for special populations. They identify the "R" and "T" components as particularly significant. Virtually all high-level users stress that educators need to greatly expand their emphasis on student's self-*reflection* and self-*regulation*. This metacognitive component, they acknowledge, is especially important for students with special needs. The more learner-centered and learner-owned the process of education becomes, the greater the likelihood that all students will realize their innate potential. Similarly, the "T" element reminds educators to *tailor* their instruction to accommodate individual student strengths and needs; this is the essence of differentiated instruction and assessment.

In general, the one-on-one interviews, focus group discussions, and questionnaires have identified the following connections between UbD and educating students with special needs:

• The universal need for rigorous core standards and the related results for all learners, not just for a select few.

• The need to unpack content standards to identify big ideas, enduring understandings, and essential questions that elicit inquiry and exploration so all students gain deep conceptual understanding.

• The need to design and implement a differentiated approach (1) to assess and identify all learners' strengths and needs; (2) to provide multiple vehicles so learners can demonstrate formative and summative achievement relative to rigorous standards; and (3) to create a learning profile for all learners so educators can modify instruction and learning experiences to accommodate students' individual learning styles, needs, and interests.

• The imperative to transcend single-faceted testing as the exclusive way to monitor student achievement.

• The critical necessity of having all teachers receive adequate professional development on the use of differentiated instruction to promote equity and excellence for all students.

The Need for Long-Term Evaluation Studies

Although practitioners contend that high levels of UbD implementation reinforce improved assessment and evaluation practices and student efficacy, they also express a common desire for valid longitudinal program evaluation data illustrating UbD's value. Increasingly, this kind of data is required for both state and federal grant funding, and local funding.

"At this point, I can only offer my firm belief [that UbD use leads to higher student achievement]. [I have] no evidence," says Egan of Virginia. Similarly, Joseph Corriero, an assistant superintendent for curriculum and instruction in Cranford, New Jersey, notes, "To date, we have no data that indicate a link between our UbD work and student achievement. We hope to pursue this investigation through our Professional Development School partnership with Seton Hall University."

In general, many high-level users express an intuitive, rather than empirical, foundation for their support of the UbD framework. A comment from Jan Zuehlke, a social studies coordinator in Willis, Texas, is typical: "I have not done a direct correlation, but I believe that UbD could help students on the state test because [UbD] requires students to think at higher levels of understanding."

Other practitioners cite a discrepancy between the design of their state accountability tests and the principles espoused by UbD. For example, Alberti of Virginia describes her experiences with accountability issues:

> Since my responsibility is for gifted education services, I find UbD to have an excellent fit with the kind of curricular and learning experiences high-ability students need based on their characteristics. Unfortunately, our local and state accountability testing is very narrowly focused and, regrettably, teaching and learning have become characteristically so.

Some respondents also mention that both the relative youth of the UbD framework and the limits on its district-level use to date make it difficult to gauge the framework's exact effect on achievement test scores. Meara of New Jersey notes, "Our standardized tests are as yet unable to be a determiner, as the units are only now being implemented." Similarly, Margaret Searle, an educational consultant in Perrysburg, Ohio, comments

> Since UbD is not a program, but principles embedded in other initiatives, I would be hard-pressed to attribute gains directly to UbD. I do know that the districts where we have had big gains have begun to think in terms of these principles as the teachers have begun to work as teams. I believe the issue of working as teams with quality techniques is where the difference lies between significant and small gains. Teachers in isolation have a tough time making significant scoring differences for a district.

Carl Zon, a standards and assessment coach and educational consultant from Sunnyvale, California, also reinforces this idea:

> It is too early in the work to have generated this kind of evidence. Consistent with the work of Hord, Rutherford, Huling-Austin, and Hall,* teachers are predominantly at the mechanical and routine levels of use. However, their efficacy is clearly beginning to improve, as they perceive increased student engagement in learning experiences as a function of UbD elements in action in their curriculum.

Joan Spratley, the director of special and gifted education for the Norfolk Public Schools in Norfolk, Virginia, underscores a similar optimism about the potential future effect of UbD use on the populations with whom she works:

> This is new territory for special education, but my belief is that we will be able to link [UbD's] usage to quality individualized educational programs for students with disabilities and their ability to successfully participate in the general education curriculum. Successful participation in the general education curriculum should lead to greater student achievement for students with disabilities.

In general, then, although practitioners are sanguine about the positive effect of UbD on their school and district assessment and evaluation practices, they are clear about the need for long-term evaluation studies of UbD's value. David Malone, senior vice president of Quality Learning in Missouri City, Texas, describes one such evaluation process:

> The comprehensive pre-assessment tools we have developed are being used by teachers on campuses this year. Follow-up surveys will be given to students and teachers at the end of each year for three years. Campuses are sending their teachers through training in three

---

Ed. note: Reference is to the Concerns-Based Adoption Model (CBAM), presented in Hord, Rutherford, Huling-Austin, & Hall (1987).

waves: "early adopters" first, then the "followers," and finally, the "change challenged." Each year, as students and teachers are surveyed about their current practices, the rankings of teachers having completed the training will be compared with the rankings of those who have not been trained on UbD.

As districts develop and implement similar studies of UbD and its effect on student achievement of curriculum standards, district leaders may wish to consider the following recommendations from high-level UbD practitioners:

• Develop district-specific profiles of UbD users to empirically confirm which assessment and instructional behaviors are associated with high levels of UbD use and implementation.

• Identify exemplary educators within the district whose professional behavior reflects the district profile for UbD use.

• Consider developing demonstration sites to showcase high-level users and present their classrooms as models for professional development and peer observation.

• Develop experimental evaluation studies in which baseline student-achievement data are established for educators who are beginning their UbD training. Include longitudinal studies of student progress in the new users' classrooms as they expand their application of UbD strategies and techniques, compared to student progress in classes where teachers are not participating in UbD training or implementation.

• From those longitudinal studies, extrapolate interventions and instructional practices that are proving effective in promoting high levels of student achievement on standardized tests. Emphasize those interventions and practices as part of districtwide professional development and strategic planning related to test score improvement.

• Reinforce administrators' understanding of research-based strategies and interventions as part of formal and informal teacher observations.

■   ■   ■

These recommendations can complement existing school and district work on strategic planning and continuous improvement. As you reflect on the implications of this chapter's recommendations and conclusions for your learning organization, you may wish to consult the following resources. The organizational assessment matrix in Figure 3.1 presents the characteristics of students in UbD-based classrooms that practitioners point to as evidence of high levels of understanding and achievement.

Increasingly, supervisory models emphasize what students do when instructors reinforce mastery of standards in learning situations that focus on understanding, not just knowledge–recall behaviors. This chapter's second organizational assessment matrix, Figure 3.2, lists universal indicators of effective assessment practices abstracted from high-level users' recommendations about UbD's Stage Two. These indicators can serve as useful and practical guidelines for all schools and districts responding to the critical issues of accountability and high-stakes testing.

3.1	**STUDENT BEHAVIORS EVIDENT IN LEARNING ENVIRONMENTS THAT PROMOTE UNDERSTANDING FOR ALL**

To what extent do student behaviors in your school or district reflect each of the following indicators?

INDICATOR	NOT EVIDENT	SOMEWHAT EVIDENT	EVIDENT	HIGHLY EVIDENT
1. All students can demonstrate a clear understanding of where they are headed and why they are going there.	☐	☐	☐	☐
2. All students can explain the purpose of a particular lesson and its key structural elements.	☐	☐	☐	☐
3. All students can describe the connection between their learning activities and the standards for which they are responsible.	☐	☐	☐	☐
4. All students can identify and explain the big ideas and essential questions that are at the heart of the content that they are studying.	☐	☐	☐	☐
5. All students can demonstrate their ability to explain and to interpret the significance of the key facts, concepts, generalizations, rules, laws, and principles that they are learning (core declarative knowledge).	☐	☐	☐	☐

Continued

INDICATOR	NOT EVIDENT	SOMEWHAT EVIDENT	EVIDENT	HIGHLY EVIDENT
6. All students can demonstrate a capacity for independently applying the skills, procedures, and processes that they are acquiring (core procedural knowledge).	☐	☐	☐	☐
7. All students can describe, analyze, and evaluate contrasting perspectives associated with controversial ideas, issues, and events that they are studying.	☐	☐	☐	☐
8. Where appropriate, all students can demonstrate empathy for individuals and groups about whom they are studying.	☐	☐	☐	☐
9. All students can demonstrate a clear understanding of the criteria being used to evaluate their achievement.	☐	☐	☐	☐
10. All students can play an active role in evaluating their own performance and its growth relative to identified standards.	☐	☐	☐	☐

Organizational Assessment

3.1 | **STUDENT BEHAVIORS EVIDENT IN LEARNING ENVIRONMENTS THAT PROMOTE UNDERSTANDING FOR ALL**

To what extent do student behaviors in your school or district reflect each of the following indicators?

INDICATOR	NOT EVIDENT	SOMEWHAT EVIDENT	EVIDENT	HIGHLY EVIDENT
11. All students can demonstrate proficiency in expressing their achievement in multiple assessment modes (e.g., tests, quizzes, academic prompts, reflections, and culminating performance-based projects).	☐	☐	☐	☐
12. All students learn actively; they can reflect on, revisit, revise, and rethink their growing knowledge, skills, and understandings.	☐	☐	☐	☐

3.2 ASSESSMENT AND EVALUATION PRACTICES THAT PROMOTE UNDERSTANDING FOR ALL

To what extent do assessment practices in your school or district reflect each of the following indicators?

INDICATOR	NOT EVIDENT	SOMEWHAT EVIDENT	EVIDENT	HIGHLY EVIDENT
1. Our core curriculum contains rigorous content and performance standards for all learners.	☐	☐	☐	☐
2. We have designed our curriculum so that teachers can monitor all students' progress and can adjust instruction to accommodate individual students' strengths and needs.	☐	☐	☐	☐
3. Our assessment clearly aligns with the desired results of our curriculum.	☐	☐	☐	☐
4. All teachers in our school or district emphasize a photo album approach to assessment, rather than a snapshot of student achievement.	☐	☐	☐	☐
5. Our tests and quizzes include constructed-response items in which students are engaged in some form of timed or untimed performance.	☐	☐	☐	☐

Continued   **Organizational Assessment**

| 3.2 | **ASSESSMENT AND EVALUATION PRACTICES THAT PROMOTE UNDERSTANDING FOR ALL** |

To what extent do assessment practices in your school or district reflect each of the following indicators?

INDICATOR	NOT EVIDENT	SOMEWHAT EVIDENT	EVIDENT	HIGHLY EVIDENT
6. Self-assessment is a major part of monitoring student progress and includes the ongoing use of journals, logs, and other reflective writings, plus peer review and coaching.	☐	☐	☐	☐
7. Rather than assigning assessment activities, our teachers present them in the form of academic prompts that identify format, audience, topic, and purpose.	☐	☐	☐	☐
8. Our students have an opportunity to engage in independent culminating performance tasks and projects.	☐	☐	☐	☐
9. Our students are active in the assessment and evaluation process, and we continuously emphasize their self-reflection and self-assessment relative to articulated standards.	☐	☐	☐	☐

Continued

INDICATOR	NOT EVIDENT	SOMEWHAT EVIDENT	EVIDENT	HIGHLY EVIDENT
10. Our testing program represents only one of multiple elements of our approach to assessing and evaluating student progress and organizational effectiveness.	☐	☐	☐	☐

4

PROMOTING STUDENT
UNDERSTANDING

ESSENTIAL QUESTIONS

1. *How can educators help all students understand the curriculum that they study?*

2. *How can Understanding by Design be a vehicle that helps educators to differentiate instruction to address the unique strengths and needs of every student?*

3. *What does a standards-based classroom look like when it reflects Understanding by Design instructional principles and strategies?*

What does it mean to teach for understanding? How can educators ensure that all students achieve this important goal? This chapter examines such questions by exploring the instructional implications of the Understanding by Design (UbD) framework and by emphasizing how successful practitioners have internalized the strategies and processes implicit in Stage Three's WHERETO template (see Chapter 1, page 19) and have then refocused these elements on their teaching practices.

Patty Isabel Cortez, an English language arts coach at Morris High School in the Bronx, New York City, powerfully underscores how UbD can transform teachers' perceptions of their roles and their approaches to instructional design. Her voice is particularly revealing in regards to UbD's role in helping educators increase their capacity to *reflect, revisit, revise,* and *rethink* their understanding of both their students and the content they are teaching:

> I recently completed my second Understanding by Design unit. Am I learning more about UbD? Frankly, I am learning more about the way I teach, the way I plan, [and] the way I align standards with literary units and texts, [plus] why I choose certain literary pieces. Creating these units has given me a magnifying glass that I use to self-assess my lessons, pedagogical approaches, and student outcomes. I find it fascinating that after 12 years of teaching, I can still be as enthusiastic about how and why I teach certain works of literature.

The "W" Element: Ensuring Students Know *Where* They Are Headed, *Why* They Are Going There, and in *What Ways* They Will Be Evaluated

Most high-level users stress the value of UbD's emphasis on making sure all students know where they are going in a particular lesson or unit and why they are going there. In addition to ensuring that learners have a focused understanding of curriculum standards, students need to understand how they will be evaluated—as well as how they will monitor and evaluate themselves—throughout an instructional episode or process.

Michael Jackson, an 8th grade language arts teacher at Grover Middle School in Princeton Junction, New Jersey, asserts

> Essential and guiding questions have had the most visible [effect] on my teaching, as well as my students' understanding and performance. On a daily basis, I'm forced to identify the purpose of every experience my students engage in. If I can't come up with a purposeful question that engages them in a search for meaning, I have to reconsider the value of the experience.

Study participants have cited a number of modifications that they have made in their instructional delivery and have noted additional examples from among the teaching practices they have observed in their respective schools and districts. Here are some of the instructional techniques that they advocate:

• Reinforce students' understanding of the purpose of a lesson or unit by helping them identify similarities and differences between and among previous activities related to the skill or subject matter they are currently learning and the learning activities in which they are presently participating.

• Determine whether students understand the purpose, goals, and objectives of the lesson or unit by asking them to summarize these in some form (orally, in writing, or through nonverbal representation).

• Establish with students a variety of ways in which their individual efforts will be reinforced and provide opportunities for recognition throughout the lesson or unit.

• Use both linguistic ways and nonlinguistic ways (e.g., nonverbal representations, flowcharts, images, and icons) to represent the purposes and key ideas of a particular lesson or unit.

• Begin a lesson or unit by grouping students into cooperative work teams that will be responsible for some form of shared inquiry, problem solving, decision making, or all three.

• Cue students into the purpose of a lesson or unit by helping them narrow their focus.

• Avoid making instructional goals too specific by incorporating big ideas, enduring understandings, and essential questions.

• Encourage students to personalize instructional goals by helping them adapt those goals to their personal needs and experiences through the use of student–teacher contracts.

- Facilitate students' generation of hypotheses and the subsequent testing of their ideas.

- Pose questions—especially big, open-ended, and interpretive questions—at the beginning of a lesson or unit to cue students into the big ideas and activate prior knowledge related to the lesson or unit.

- Use cues and questions to help students focus on what is important, rather than what is unusual.

- Use advance organizers to represent relevant introductory materials before learning begins; each organizer should present introductory materials, ideas, and related information at a higher level of abstraction, generality, and inclusiveness than the information presented after it.

- Use various types of advance organizers (e.g., expository, narrative, and skimming) to help students focus on what is important, particularly with information that may not be initially well organized or easily accessible to the learner.

The "H" Element: *Hooking* Student Interest in and Ownership of the Learning Process

Educators today express increasing concern about students' lack of interest in the learning process. High-level users confirm that the instructional principles underlying Stage Three are conducive to promoting students' sense of engagement in and ownership of their own learning. Consider this comment from Scott Berger, an 8th grade social studies teacher in Princeton Junction, New Jersey:

> In regard to backward design, I feel it helps [if] teachers and students focus attention on what is important and then pursue it for deeper investigation. This provides different check-in points ([from] guiding question [to] essential question [to] to course questions) [as] a form of scaffolding that lets us connect different concepts and understandings to make the whole picture clearer. It also lends itself

to creating worldly problem-solving opportunities, and this helps to engage students and lets them find relevance for the class in their lives. Also, backward design is set up for easy reflection and revision, in that it is continually asking questions about its effectiveness and success. This is the essence of education.

Cortez of New York City describes how UbD has reinforced the importance of cueing into students' interests, backgrounds, and experiences when designing learning activities:

> My first unit, which is based on Chaucer's "The Franklin's Tale," includes some of the following understandings: "Marriage and relationships are lifelong processes" and "Negotiation requires respect, honesty, and a profound awareness of the situation." I was a bit more daring in my second UbD unit, on Tennessee Williams's plays! This second unit's understandings are "Our families of our childhood influence the way we form our families as adults" and "A family has to govern itself through clear communication, accountability, and a system of checks and balances."
>
> Why am I delving into these particular understandings? Essentially, I believe they address our students' immediate needs. Our "at-risk" students not only need to pass the [English language arts] Regents, but [also], most imperatively, need to learn to cope with the issues that accompany poverty and alienation within and outside the family structure. I feel grateful that my own academic background helps me to merge classical literature and the urgent and pertinent issues that our students face every day of their lives.

The following recommendations reflect the range of suggestions and observations high-level users have made concerning the "H" element in instructional design:

• Engage students' interest and involvement at the beginning of a lesson by having them create metaphors or analogies to reflect their familiarity with and understanding of a lesson's topic or issue.

• Promote students' participation through reciprocal teaching activities that begin the lesson and are revisited throughout it.

• Establish rules, processes, and symbols to be used for recognition and rewards that are contingent on the attainment of some standard of performance.

• Stimulate students' imagination by having them create nonverbal representations, physical models, mental pictures, or pictographs at the beginning of a lesson, and revisit these later as students enhance their knowledge, skills, and understandings.

• Warm up students' enthusiasm through some form of advance organizer, introductory cooperative learning interaction, or activity.

• Ask students to engage in some form of K-W-L to personalize objectives and the learning process (i.e., What do I think I know about this subject? What do I want to learn about it? At the conclusion of this lesson, what have I learned?).

• Cue students into the big ideas of a lesson or unit by posing an essential question and having students respond to it.

The First "E" Element: *Equipping* Students for Success Through *Experience*-Based Learning

High-level users also emphasize the need to encourage student exploration, experience, and inquiry into the big ideas and essential questions underlying the content they are studying. This comment, from Jackson of New Jersey, is typical:

> The need to contextualize experiences has been a springboard for research on my part as to why I teach certain concepts [or] skills. In my struggles to establish a purpose for using the conventions of punctuation in my 8th grade language arts class, I began to engage in conversations with colleagues and supervisors to discuss *why* they

teach such conventions. These discussions gave me greater insight into the connections between mechanics and craftsmanship. Seemingly sophisticated but fundamentally decontextualized questions, such as "How does the dependency of clauses affect the use of commas?" have evolved into more meaningful questions, such as "How does comma usage contribute to clarity?" "How does the use or misuse of punctuation and sentence structure help a writer to find his or her voice?" and "How is *less-is-more* exemplified by the intentional use of sentence fragments?"

The first of the "E" elements in Stage Three's WHERETO instructional design template focuses on encouraging learners' direct *experience* of curriculum standards and content. Such strategies *equip* students to pursue their own inquiry into core knowledge, skills, and understandings. This element of UbD's instructional design process elicited the greatest number of recommended strategies and tactics from study participants, including the following:

• Present similarities and differences both in verbal and linguistic formats and in nonverbal and symbolic formats.

• Make summarizing and note taking a direct and ongoing part of instructional delivery; encourage students to analyze information at a deep level and to delete, substitute, and keep information based on their analysis.

• Use a variety of summarizing strategies and frameworks.

• Coach students in effective note taking: a mixture of informal outlines, webbing, and combination techniques (e.g., the three-column note approach).

• Emphasize abstract (rather than concrete) forms of recognition to reinforce effort; find ongoing opportunities to acknowledge successful or outstanding work progress and use peer response and feedback options.

- Personalize praise when possible through techniques such as the ongoing use of the "pause, prompt, and praise" strategy.

- Ensure that homework is a meaningful complement to and extension of classroom activities and learning and that it has a clearly stated purpose and outcome.

- Establish homework protocols: (1) set and communicate a homework policy, (2) always reinforce the purpose of and evaluation criteria for homework, and (3) vary feedback approaches.

- Provide appropriate and continuing opportunities for students to practice and rehearse their procedural knowledge (i.e., skills, procedures, and processes); use approaches such as (1) focused practice with extensive coaching, (2) opportunities to adapt to and shape newly acquired knowledge, and (3) sustained movement toward independent use and application.

- Reinforce students' mastery of essential procedural knowledge through practices such as (1) charting accuracy and speed, (2) designing practice assignments that focus on specific elements of a complex skill or process, and (3) planning time for students to increase their conceptual understanding of skills and processes.

- Support students' acquisition and integration of essential knowledge through nonlinguistic representations such as (1) using graphic organizers, (2) building physical models, (3) generating mental pictures, and (4) drawing pictures and pictographs.

- Whenever possible, integrate physical movement and related kinesthetic activities to promote student ownership of curriculum content.

- Promote students' processing of key information and skills through cooperative learning activities that (1) use a variety of criteria for grouping students; (2) include informal, formal, and base groups; and (3) are used consistently and systematically without overuse.

• Integrate a coaching approach to provide feedback that is timely, corrective in nature, and specific to an evaluation criterion.

• Provide students with extensive opportunities to self-assess and to participate in peer-response group activities, so that they can practice giving criterion-referenced feedback and tailoring feedback for specific types of knowledge and skills.

• Encourage students to generate and test hypotheses in various settings: from the natural sciences to social studies to reading for deep understanding.

• Reinforce students' support of claims, assertions, and conclusions with valid and complete evidence by (1) providing students with templates for reporting and explaining their work; (2) providing sentence stems for students—especially young students—to help them articulate their explanations; (3) providing—or developing with students—rubrics that clarify the evaluation criteria for their explanations; and (4) setting up opportunities for students to defend and orally explain their hypotheses and explanations.

• Teach students—directly and consistently—how to respond to and understand higher-level questions, including questions that require inferences and deductions (i.e., about things, people, actions, and states of being) and analysis (i.e., analyzing perspectives, analyzing errors, and constructing support).

• Use enduring understandings and essential questions as cueing devices to frame students' inquiry and exploration of big ideas and concepts.

• Integrate advance organizers into all aspects of instructional delivery to help students cue into what is important and significant for them to retain and to understand.

The "R" Element and Metacognition: *Reflecting, Revisiting, Revising,* and *Rethinking*

Effective learning extends from students' ability to monitor their own learning process. This big idea is a central theme in high-level users' comments on the next phase of the WHERETO template. Jackson of New Jersey summarizes his renewed emphasis on student reflection and revision in relationship to his work with UbD in this way:

> [E]ssential questions and guiding questions have brought this former primary teacher back to the constructivist practice of Socratic questioning. Metaphorical phrasing of questions seems to be a highly effective means to get learners to look at each experience as a child would look at a puzzle or a specimen—with inquisitive intellectual curiosity. When faced with the question, "If Character and Plot were Spiderman and the Green Goblin, who would win the Battle Royal?" learners become engaged in a debate over which story element is more powerful, only to be carefully guided to the realization that [Character and Plot] are codependent, like Batman and Robin. Essential questions and guiding questions are the superheroes of UbD.

Study participants have identified various strategies and tools for promoting students' capacity for reflecting, revisiting, revising, and rethinking their learning process. As the following recommendations reinforce, the "R" element of WHERETO aligns itself powerfully with concepts such as metacognition and comprehension monitoring, which are essential elements of a balanced literacy model.

• Get students to look for patterns in the lesson or unit (e.g., big ideas, themes, recurrent issues, unresolved conflicts, and perspectives) and to find ways to classify the patterns according to their common attributes.

• Help students to synthesize their learning and to reinforce their understanding through summarizing and note taking using both linguistic and nonlinguistic representations.

• Help students to reinforce their own effort and to recognize their own progress through metacognitive tools such as reflective journals, think logs, and peer response groups.

• Use homework as a vehicle for students' independent application and refinement of the work they have done in class.

• Organize cooperative learning cohorts at the conclusion of lessons and units to allow students to summarize, reflect, revisit, and refine their shared perceptions and conclusions about curriculum content.

• Have students revisit big ideas, enduring understandings, and essential questions as closure activities for lessons and units.

The Second "E" Element: Student Self-*Evaluation* and Self-*Expression*

Carl Zon, a standards and assessment coach and educational consultant in Sunnyvale, California, synthesizes what most high-level users suggest about the contributions of student self-evaluation and self-expression:

> Teachers need to [make] students aware at the outset of the expected standards and levels of performance related to a culminating performance task, [thus] getting students to know they are applying what they have learned or are learning something they will use to do something else (transfer).

> Using scoring guides [gives] students specific formative and summative feedback and [allows] them time to use the feedback to self-correct and self-adjust, [thereby] getting students to self-reflect in some way that exhibits evidence of content area and lifelong learning.

High-level users offer varied recommendations for reinforcing students' self-expression and self-regulation, but they generally agree on the following strategies:

• Encourage students to compare their pre- and post-progress as they move through a lesson or unit (e.g., How am I now compared to how I was when I started?).

• Have students self-evaluate by assessing the extent to which they perceive themselves as mastering identified objectives.

• Help students self-evaluate in product-based ways (with written products, logs, and journals) and dialogue-based ways (with listen-think-pair-share activities, small-group feedback sessions, and peer response groups); have them assess the extent to which they perceive themselves as mastering identified content standards and performance objectives.

• Ask students to express in written, oral, and visual formats their perceptions and evaluations of how they are doing relative to mastering lesson, unit, or course objectives.

• Help students to complete complex reasoning processes (e.g., systems analysis, problem solving, decision making, investigation, and experimental inquiry) by applying class rubrics to their own work and that of their peers.

The "T" Element: *Tailoring* Teaching to Fit the Needs of All Learners

Differentiated instruction is an emerging priority in education. Although the term *differentiated instruction* has various meanings for educators, it usually entails the big idea that educators must continually assess and monitor all students' strengths and needs relative to accountability standards. It also emphasizes modifying and adjusting instruction to accommodate students' identified strengths and needs. The following comment from Zon of California, discussing the challenges of differentiating instruction and assessment in the classroom, represents the view of most high-level users:

Teachers are struggling with these things: identifying big ideas; having available models of student work as guides; covering content versus focusing on in-depth learning, given the time it takes (less is more); writing task-specific scoring guides from a generic scoring guide (rubric); and getting a handle on the elements of a complex process [of] templates, standards, indicators, lessons that provide opportunities to learn, levels of performance, and descriptions of quality.

The "T" element of WHERETO, which requires that teachers *tailor* learning activities to accommodate assessed student needs, elicits various recommendations from high-level users:

• Use a variety of formative assessments (e.g., tests or quizzes, reflective assessments, academic prompts, performance tasks) to determine where students are as they begin the lesson or unit; help them to self-classify according to their specific strengths, needs, and interests.

• Review with students (individually, in small groups, as a whole group) their summarizing and note-taking processes related to key lesson or unit information and skills; use emergent issues and problems as tools for reteaching and revisiting material as needed.

• Throughout the lesson or unit, find ways to reinforce effort and to provide recognition related to students' individual progress and achievement of their personal best.

• Integrate one-on-one and small-group coaching opportunities as students rehearse, practice, and apply independently the knowledge and skills that they are acquiring.

• Use students' creation of nonlinguistic representations (e.g., graphic organizers, models, pictographs) of the material they are learning as a vehicle for identifying and addressing their emergent strengths, needs, and misunderstandings.

• Balance cooperative learning cohorts to ensure that all students can express their respective strengths, needs, and talents.

• Use a variety of tools and media to provide ongoing feedback to students concerning their progress toward mastering lesson and unit objectives; allow students to help create and apply rubrics and scoring tools.

• Observe and assess students' response to instructional cues, questions, and follow-up probes to determine when individuals need special assistance or coaching to correct misunderstandings and errors.

The "O" Element: *Organizing* for Success to Promote Students' Capacity for Independent Application

Finally, according to high-level users, effective instruction and learning require careful organization of learning activities. Specifically, this process entails moving students from initial concrete experiences toward growing levels of conceptual understanding and independent application. According to Zon of California:

> [As a result of Understanding by Design use], teachers are beginning to do these things: [design] culminating tasks that ask students to show how they are performing on no more than three selected standards and indicators, [teach] a backward-planned unit as a foundation for a culminating task, [design] complex tasks with lifelong learning standards in mind, [become] more reflective about their practice, and [open] up their classrooms and themselves to coaching to enhance their practice.

High-level users agree that the following strategies and interventions are key to organizing instruction and learning activities to promote high levels of student achievement:

• Help students to compare how they are growing in their understanding from the beginning to the end of the lesson or unit.

• Use a variety of formats (e.g., outlines or webbing) to establish a road map of the lesson or unit for students to follow.

• Begin a unit with a "town meeting" to establish priorities and ways for students to monitor their own effort; hold follow-up meetings to reinforce effort.

• Organize the teaching of procedural knowledge (skills, procedures, and processes) so that students move from teacher-directed modeling toward a growing independent shaping and rehearsal, which will culminate in some form of independent product or performance.

• Structure units so that lessons help students move toward independent application of complex cognitive processes such as systems analysis, problem solving, decision making, investigation, invention, or experimental inquiry.

• Help students to demonstrate a growing proficiency and independent understanding through increasingly complex assessments, which will culminate in some form of real-world, independent performance task or project.

• Organize learning so that students grow in their ability to demonstrate and to assess increasing levels of independent use of one or more of the six facets of understanding: explanation, interpretation, application, perspective, empathy, and self-knowledge.

■   ■   ■

The detailed participant responses presented in this chapter testify to the value and range of Stage Three instructional strategies and interventions. Some of the end-of-chapter resources may be helpful as you consider these recommendations for your own classroom, school, or district. Figure 4.1 concentrates this chapter's suggestions into a relatively brief overview of major themes and strategies. The organizational assessment matrix represented in Figure 4.2 extrapolates core UbD instructional principles and strategies for use in general strategic and school improvement planning.

4.1 | GENERAL OBSERVATIONS ABOUT AND STRATEGIES FOR TEACHING FOR UNDERSTANDING

1. Teaching to promote deep conceptual understanding requires that teachers deeply understand the content that they are teaching. This competency allows them to help students identify and explore the big ideas and essential questions at the heart of the program, subject, course, or unit.

2. Students acquire deep understanding when they have the time to discuss, explore, and inquire, thereby constructing meaning for themselves rather than being told the meaning.

3. When students understand content, they model and apply the thinking processes and habits of mind used by practitioners. For example, a historian compares primary source documents, infers patterns of interconnection among historical events, and acquires relevant and complete evidence to support claims and assertions. Students who understand history reflect these same processes and habits.

4. Teachers who promote deep comprehension integrate the six facets of understanding (explanation, interpretation, application, perspective, empathy, and self-knowledge) into daily classroom delivery. They also determine which facets most appropriately reinforce students' understanding in a given setting or context.

5. The six facets of understanding are not hierarchical or taxonomical. They deserve equal weight and reflect parallel complexity.

6. The most complex and difficult part of teaching for understanding entails educators' ability to create enduring understandings and essential questions. Frequently, teachers are trained to see the "trees," not the "forest," in content; therefore, they may have difficulty seeing the big picture of a program, subject, course, or unit.

7. Teaching for understanding requires a seamless connection between instruction and assessment. Educators are always in assessment mode as they modify what they do and what they have students do and as they collect evidence about students' emerging strengths and needs.

Continued

4.1	**GENERAL OBSERVATIONS ABOUT AND STRATEGIES FOR TEACHING FOR UNDERSTANDING**

8. Students develop deep conceptual understanding when they can

   • Articulate why they are doing what they are being asked to do.

   • Experience a sense of ownership and purposefulness in their learning activities.

   • Explore big ideas and essential questions instead of focusing on discrete knowledge taught in isolation.

   • Receive the mentoring and coaching they need to successfully complete all required assessments.

   • Demonstrate a growing capacity for self-reflection and self-evaluation.

   • Have their instruction modified according to their expressed needs and interests.

   • Experience instruction that integrates concrete experiences and inquiry with attention to concepts, generalizations, rules, and processes.

4.2 INSTRUCTIONAL PRACTICES THAT PROMOTE EXCELLENCE, EQUITY, AND UNDERSTANDING FOR ALL

To what extent do instructional practices in your school or district reflect each of the following indicators?

INDICATOR	NOT EVIDENT	SOMEWHAT EVIDENT	EVIDENT	HIGHLY EVIDENT
1. Teachers emphasize unit design, rather than discrete or isolated lessons; they put the learner at the center of the learning process.	☐	☐	☐	☐
2. Students receive ongoing support to understand where they are headed, why they are going there, and in what ways they will be evaluated.	☐	☐	☐	☐
3. At key junctures, students participate in activities that engage and hook their interest and imagination.	☐	☐	☐	☐
4. Teachers emphasize experiential learning that allows students to engage in exploration and inquiry.	☐	☐	☐	☐
5. Teachers encourage students to reflect, revisit, revise, and rethink their knowledge and growing understanding.	☐	☐	☐	☐

4.2 | INSTRUCTIONAL PRACTICES THAT PROMOTE EXCELLENCE, EQUITY, AND UNDERSTANDING FOR ALL

To what extent do instructional practices in your school or district reflect each of the following indicators?

INDICATOR	NOT EVIDENT	SOMEWHAT EVIDENT	EVIDENT	HIGHLY EVIDENT
6. Students have regular opportunities for self-evaluation and self-expression.	☐	☐	☐	☐
7. Using ongoing monitoring and assessment, teachers modify their approach in order to accommodate students' unique strengths and needs.	☐	☐	☐	☐
8. Teachers organize learning experiences so that students progress from concrete experiences to abstract conceptualization to independent understanding, as demonstrated through an ability to explain, interpret, and apply learning in new or unanticipated situations and settings.	☐	☐	☐	☐

5

PROMOTING EXEMPLARY PROFESSIONAL DEVELOPMENT PROGRAMS AND PRACTICES

ESSENTIAL QUESTIONS

1. *To what extent do the principles and strategies of Understanding by Design apply to all facets of professional development?*

2. *What can educators do to promote adult learners' genuine understanding in training and related staff development situations?*

3. *How can long-term users of Understanding by Design provide insights about exemplary programs and practices for professional development?*

4. *How can electronic resources complement school and district efforts to implement Understanding by Design?*

Probably the single most significant and consistent conclusion among all high-level users is that professional development plays a critical role in promoting and sustaining successful Understanding by Design (UbD) implementation. What have successful practitioners discovered about the best approaches to training and professional development related to implementing UbD? Specifically, their responses have centered around three major understandings:

1. One-shot training sessions, even those designed to last more than one day, cannot ensure successful organizational use of UbD.

2. Many UbD professional development programs fail to involve all stakeholders, particularly school-based administrators and central-office curriculum supervisors.

3. Successful UbD training designs must be clearly and fully aligned with other school and district initiatives and must be sustained by ongoing study groups and action research processes.

Avoiding Staff Development Pitfalls

High-level users are universally adamant about the need for long-term commitment to Understanding by Design and the avoidance of so-called prison-training models. In effect, providing up-front sessions with no follow-up ensures that little long-term effect or sustainability will be present in staff members' work with UbD. High-level users also generally agree that small, intimate cohort trainings are preferable to large, impersonal ones, especially in light of the need for active coaching and feedback throughout the unit design process.

"Small-group participation has proven most effective," comments Kay Egan, senior coordinator for special and gifted education services in the Norfolk Public Schools, Norfolk, Virginia. Her colleague, Deborah Jo Alberti, assistant director of special and gifted education services, confirms this perspective:

> In my opinion, the most effective staff development activities have been those conducted with small, interested, and "informed" groups, groups that understand [the] principles of teaching and learning upon which to build for UbD.
>
> Regrettably, the least effective [staff development activity] has been the attempt to "spray" someone at every school and throughout the central office departments, because the interest and buy-in were not

there initially, and we haven't been able to provide the necessary support as follow-up where there was interest and buy-in. I would advise beginning with a general overview but training a small, committed group that might generate a few demonstration sites, whether entire schools or individual teachers. Having a cadre of individuals who had "dug" deep into UbD [and] who could then serve as coaches to support the demo sites would provide a more hopeful picture for deeper and truer UbD implementation. ˑ

The various specific staff development problems identified by respondents have tended to cluster around 10 basic themes, which are summarized in Figure 5.1 at the end of this chapter. Although each item on the list represents a distinct and significant potential problem in professional development generally and in UbD professional development specifically, all items reflect a failure to use the three stages of backward design. There is an absence of clearly articulated, desired end results; a failure to determine evidence of added value; and an overall lack of attention to participant understanding and the direct use of the UbD framework in daily practice.

Involving All Stakeholders

High-level users assert that, like effective instructional design, effective professional development must take into account the specific needs, backgrounds, and prior learning of participants, and must use appropriate training strategies and processes to accommodate the strengths and needs of specific learners. Another universal issue of professional development cited by all high-level users is the fundamental need for everyone in a learning organization to be involved in ongoing training and inquiry. For example, David Malone, senior vice president of Quality Learning in Missouri City, Texas, emphasizes that

A full implementation of UbD needs administrative support and buy-in, as well as teacher support. Everyone within the system needs to understand the concepts of backward design, including the campus principal. If a comprehensive planning and implementation initiative is not rolled out, principals can continue to complete teacher appraisals as they have before. Teaching effectively using backward design is a much more sophisticated approach to teaching and learning. Everyone needs to understand the difference.

Interestingly, a majority of high-level users have suggested that a problem with the design of their initial UbD training was its dependence on the engagement and involvement of "cheerleader" teachers, who were not available to provide school-based follow-up support or coaching. There is a consensus that training cohorts should be composed of at least one administrator and one teacher within the school building who are ready and able to share their experiences with others in their grade level or department. According to many high-level users, the most viable approach represents a form of "differentiated staff development," in which multiple training and development experiences are available to accommodate specific individual and group needs, thereby helping to ensure viable institutionalization of the UbD framework.

For example, Joseph Corriero, assistant superintendent for curriculum and instruction in Cranford, New Jersey, comments, "Our district is committed to UbD implementation, and we currently offer seminars, study groups, and curriculum design teams to support this work. Our seminar series has proven to be very effective." As Corriero describes, the process of ensuring organizational coherence also involves sustained attention to aligning Understanding by Design with other school and district accountability programs and activities:

> UbD serves as the hub around which we tie together district initiatives. It is part of our long-range plan, and it has been widely accepted as the preferred planning model. Administrators have to present a clear and focused vision regarding the central place of UbD work in the district's overall philosophy.

Similarly, Carl Zon, a standards and assessment coach and educational consultant in Sunnyvale, California, describes his district's engagement of key stakeholders and its commitment to organizational alignment:

> We have two cohorts of secondary teachers (70 total) who are engaged in unit design, delivery, and evaluation in the Santa Clara Unified School District. In the initial year of work, we provided three days of training and then individual coaching follow-up. In this second year of work, many of our initial cohort members are serving as liaisons to support site-level work in teams. We provided two four-hour evening sessions to support liaisons and one and one-half days of additional training and team collaboration time. Each of the secondary schools has a modest amount of site-level collaboration time as well. Secondary administrators have also participated in training sessions and are expected to support site-level work, with coaching support from the district.

In general, high-level users recommend the following practices to ensure the involvement of all school or district stakeholders in UbD implementation:

• Integrate Understanding by Design with other district accountability initiatives to ensure that participants do not perceive it as "one more thing to do."

• Make certain that all training cohorts involve a microcosm of the learning community being served, particularly administrators responsible for coaching, observing, and evaluating team members.

• Encourage participants to see the alignment between and among UbD principles and other instructional, assessment, and professional development initiatives.

• Ensure that all units that evolve as part of ongoing professional development receive sufficient review, particularly through a coaching-based process of peer review, and that exemplary units are available for all staff members to examine and, where appropriate, to use as part of their curriculum delivery process.

• Examine ways in which UbD strategies and practices are already consistent with the lesson or unit design principles and observation templates used within the school or district.

• Wherever possible, focus on the potential relationship between high levels of UbD use and student achievement targets within the continuous improvement plan of the school or district.

Addressing the Needs of the Adult Learner and Inevitable Stages of Concern

Experienced UbD users also point out the need to address the inevitable cognitive dissonance that accompanies a powerful organizational change catalyst like Understanding by Design. From the perspective of the adult learner, the UbD framework often appears to trigger the following concerns and accompanying questions:

• *Concern about the availability of time.* How am I supposed to do this when I have so much to get through? When will I find the time to do this and still complete everything else that I am responsible for?

• *Concern about the curriculum.* This makes sense, but our curriculum is so full of standards that we have to cover the content quickly to touch on everything that's required by the state or district. How can we possibly teach for deep understanding?

• *Anxiety about testing programs.* What if I teach this way and my test scores go down? I have to make certain that I cover everything on the state assessments.

• *Concern about student ability.* This is fine for gifted students, but what about students who lack basic skills? How is this going to benefit them?

- *Fears about student expectations and behavior.* Most of my students just want me to give them the answers. How can I get them to be interested in exploring open-ended questions and dealing with topics in depth?

- *Lack of deep understanding of the discipline or content area.* I've been assigned to teach this, but I don't have a solid background in it. This isn't really my field of expertise. How am I supposed to deal with deep understanding when I'm not really comfortable with the content myself?

- *Apprehension about new methods and approaches.* For years I've been planning for what my students are going to do the next day. Why can't I start with activities and let the standards get woven into them? Why does UbD make such a big deal about unit design when our district emphasizes lesson planning?

- *Feeling like the odd one out.* I'm one of the few people in my school who is trained in UbD. What do I do about everyone else using more old-fashioned or traditional methods?

- *Apprehension about administrative support.* None of my administrators have gotten any training in UbD. What do I do when one of them observes me and doesn't understand why my students are debating questions and exploring big ideas rather than just receiving direct instruction in basic content?

- *"Been there, done that" and "This too shall pass."* This isn't anything new. Weren't we doing this kind of teaching back in the '60s? My district tends to hop on bandwagons and fads. How do I know this won't be just another flavor of the month?

While preparing to respond to these and other questions, school and district leaders who are implementing UbD must also be prepared to facilitate participants' movement through inevitable stages of concern and growth, as described in Sparks (1999), Sparks and Hirsh

(1997), and Guskey (2002). High-level users of UbD have tended to identify a common pattern of learning about and internalizing the UbD framework. Although every individual is different, those who move toward high-level use and genuine ownership of the UbD framework typically go through the following stages of progression.

Stage 1: Initial Investigation of Framework Elements and Design Principles

Successful beginning practitioners of UbD make a sincere effort to internalize the big ideas of the framework (e.g., the three-circle audit process, backward design and its three stages, the six facets of understanding, and areas of alignment with other school and district practices). In the initial phases of work with unit design, most high-level users report initial satisfaction with the first-try unit results, but they share an internal drive to be less self-conscious and more automatic about using UbD principles to design units.

Stage 2: Cognitive Dissonance Involving Prior and Current Learning

High-level users report that inevitably, and often simultaneously with initial segues into unit design, they and most of their peers experience a tension between the design principles and requirements for successfully developing a UbD unit and their own prior professional learning and experiences. Citing many of the concerns and issues listed previously, UbD practitioners report a certain amount of frustration when trying to reconcile their previous training in lesson design, assessment, and instruction with the requirements of teaching for deep understanding. When individuals come to the UbD framework with previous training or experience in critical-thinking strategies, differentiated instruction, and other forms of constructivist teaching and learning, their sense of struggle or dissonance is less evident or disturbing. Generally, high-level users identify the following UbD elements as the ones that present the greatest initial challenge:

- Reconciling and aligning school or district models of lesson design with UbD's emphasis on the unit as the focus for instructional planning.

- Overcoming apprehension about state testing and a perceived need to cover or touch on all curriculum standards equally in the event that those standards show up on state tests.

- Learning to create enduring understandings that represent declarations of big ideas and of recurrent and spiraling insights at the heart of the curriculum instead of turning these understandings into variations of goals and objectives.

- Framing essential questions that are genuinely open ended, interpretive, and philosophically engaging, as well as dealing with concerns about students' resistance to curriculum elements that are divergent, not convergent.

- Struggling to understand how they will find the time to allow for student inquiry and independent work with culminating GRASPS performance tasks and projects (see Chapter 1, page 18).

- Working to align their understanding of WHERETO principles (see Chapter 1, page 19) as the blueprint for instructional design, rather than as a template for lesson plans.

- Overcoming anxiety about the universal application of UbD principles and processes to all students, which is a variation of the misperception that UbD works for gifted or highly able students, but not for underachievers or students with special needs.

Stage 3: Mechanical Syntheses of Unit Design Components

This stage generally emerges when practitioners have completed their first unit and are making plans to implement it in the classroom or in a professional development setting. There appears to be a baseline comfort level with the framework's elements, but also a simultaneous struggle to remember all the elements and, particularly, to explain to others how those elements are interrelated and interconnected. The more extensive the practitioner's experience explaining and applying UbD, the greater degree of spontaneity and self-expression the practitioner reports.

Stage 4: Struggle to Internalize and Integrate Major Design Elements

As users of UbD continue to participate in follow-up professional development accompanied by ongoing use of the UbD framework in daily practice, they begin to experience a more unified understanding of the design principles and implications for venues beyond their own immediate professional setting. Most high-level users have identified this stage as the point at which they began to work with others in their school or district to integrate the entire framework—or key elements of UbD, such as the essential questions—into more expansive focus areas, such as curriculum design. Early adopters and pioneers, in particular, tend to describe this phase as both exciting and frustrating in light of existing organizational norms and practices.

Stage 5: Collaboration to Solve Problems and Celebrate Successes

For those who move from novice to successful high-level user, the next stage of development involves collaboration and some form of shared inquiry. In either a formal or informal way, practitioners begin to share their UbD experiences and invite peer feedback. This phase can be as simple as two teachers sharing materials and suggestions about ways to try out new ideas and strategies, or it can involve the more formal processes of lesson study and action research. None of the successful high-level users report having moved through the process of UbD implementation alone; some form of communal learning seems necessary to sustain and to institutionalize UbD.

Stage 6: Revisiting the Framework with Deeper Understanding

Like all models of educational change, successful UbD implementation requires that users revisit its principles and strategies with growing levels of understanding and use. High-level users note that as they gained experience implementing the model, their ability to explain the framework and its related research principles increased. They became increasingly comfortable applying UbD in their own professional settings and modifying their understanding of the framework to fit immediate classroom or administrative needs. Most strikingly, they report having grown in their capacity to interpret their curriculum, to unpack standards, and to help their students understand, not just repeat, the performance indicators associated with those standards. With experience, UbD practitioners' capacity for self-assessment and self-regulation expands in relation to the model, as does their ability to empathize with and analyze conflicting perspectives being articulated by colleagues as they progress through their own professional development. This phase involves a very clear and overt tendency to model and share with fellow professionals those units and strategies that have worked.

Stage 7: Automaticity and Alignment

Although all interviewees continue on the path toward fully internalizing UbD, high-level users tend to describe a sense of automaticity about their use of it. That is, they have become more comfortable spontaneously describing and applying its key components. They are also more fluent in articulating how the UbD framework supports and aligns with other school and district accountability initiatives. This growing internalization of UbD is best reflected in the virtually universal phenomenon of high-level users being active staff developers for the framework. Whether training others in how to use it for assessment and curriculum development or showcasing success stories from their own practice at the school level, successful users always integrate UbD into their work with organization development and continuous improvement.

Stage 8: Expansion to Organizational Implementation

The final phase of high-level users' development is the expansion of their professional work with UbD to some form of organizational application. This work can range from a leadership role on a school improvement committee to district- or state-level leadership that involves groups responsible for systemic staff development, accountability testing, and curriculum and assessment. Although high-level users reinforce their individual professional work with UbD, they also emphasize the need to share it and institutionalize it. They also reiterate the need to present it to staff and district leaders as a complement to overall accountability initiatives, rather than as a stand-alone program that may be perceived as just one more program to do.

Although these eight phases of growth are predictable and, as high-level users suggest, inevitable, they are not necessarily linear or sequential. All the expert UbD practitioners who participated in this study noted that they struggled to make personal sense of UbD and to share its potential benefits with others. That process of sharing involves another key element of successful framework implementation—creating a community committed to understanding and applying Understanding by Design.

Promoting Communities of Learning

Overall, high-level users advocate differentiated staff development that involves all stakeholders and aligns with other school and district accountability initiatives, thus reinforcing the idea of building communities of learning. Specifically, such communities focus on change variables (such as UbD) as catalysts for altering and improving overall organizational culture and operations. Like the research associated with this concept, communities of inquiry and learning share the following characteristics:

1. A consensus-driven vision and mission that is related to improved student achievement along with students' emerging roles as lifelong learners, citizens, and workers.

2. Clearly articulated organizational structures that help all stakeholders to promote and achieve this shared vision and commitment.

3. Short- and long-term performance goals and measurable objectives that allow staff members to monitor their achievement of organizational targets.

4. Active engagement of all staff members in the process of self-reflection and self-inquiry through their use of three interrelated structural processes:

a. *Study Groups:* Collections of individuals who agree to discuss and reflect on a shared collection of readings and related resources. Most high-level users cite the original *Understanding by Design* text (Wiggins & McTighe, 1998) as their entry point for exploring this framework with other staff members.

b. *Inquiry Teams:* Extensions of study groups in which interested members begin to take what they have learned and to explore potential ways in which strategies, techniques, and principles might be applied to various student achievement issues and organizational effectiveness targets.

c. *Action Research Cohorts:* The logical extension of the first two processes, action research cohorts take identified organizational problems and create and implement action plans to address them, including (1) forming a research problem or question, (2) collecting and displaying initial data related to the problem or question, (3) generating and implementing an action with clearly articulated goals and objectives for addressing the problem or question, and (4) continually modifying the plan on the basis of emerging assessment and evaluation data generated during the action research cycle.

Lynne Meara, supervisor of instruction and gifted and talented coordinator for the Plumsted Township School District in New Egypt, New Jersey, describes her district's approach to creating a UbD community of learning:

> At this point, it has become necessary to differentiate our staff development options. We have new staff orientation programs in place that involve classroom management, planning, and instruction and also their mentoring obligations. There were [staff members who] were getting coaching areas that pertained more to classroom performance than to design [and] whose needs had to be met. Our special education teachers also had responsibilities that could take them away from the design process. We tried to accommodate all of these different interest groups without diluting the integrity of the initial plan.

Similarly, Mark Wise, a social studies supervisor from Grover Middle School in Princeton Junction, New Jersey, asserts that

> The most effective [staff development] has been the consistent work with motivated and engaged teachers, who are able to constantly reflect on their practice and implement well-crafted UbD units. As well, we have used this group to model Japanese lesson studies, where they co-plan a lesson and observe each other teaching, and then provide feedback to improve the lesson and implement the revised lesson.

Jill Levine, Judy Solovey, and Joyce Tatum, key leaders at the Normal Park Museum Magnet School, Chattanooga, Tennessee, express similar sentiments about creating communities of inquiry using UbD:

The most effective professional development has been the quarterly planning days when we design the work for the next nine-week unit. We teach all social studies and science through UbD units. We also have a quarterly theme that guides our planning through understandings and essential questions across grade levels and brings us together as a school. At the end of the day, we meet as a faculty to share our Stage One and Stage Two plans, including our exhibit for the end of the term.

Electronic Communities of Learning

A majority of respondents agree that building an electronic learning community offers great potential for expanding professional understanding and use of UbD within their schools and districts. As suggested, electronic tools can help staffs to provide meaningful follow-up to initial trainings through study groups, inquiry teams, and action research projects. These tools can also enhance educators' efforts to introduce new staff members, particularly educators new to the profession, to the possibilities offered by the framework for enhancing classroom management and instructional design.

The UbD Exchange

Without question, the most widely used electronic professional development resource related to Understanding by Design is the UbD Exchange, an electronic database offering a range of services and resources. Available in both individual subscriber and district-level formats, the Exchange includes

• A rich variety of readings and explanations of various UbD elements.

• Descriptions of training workshops available to prospective and current UbD users and a workshop calendar.

• A PowerPoint presentation providing an overview of the UbD framework and course maps.

• A glossary of terms associated with Understanding by Design and its use.

• A database with accompanying search engine that allows users to access more than 2,500 UbD units, including exemplary units (identified by a Gold Cup or Blue Ribbon icon) reviewed by UbD cadre members and units-in-progress submitted by individuals who have posted them online as part of the Exchange.

• An electronic framework for online UbD unit development, including an option for the users to request feedback on their units from UbD cadre members.

• Curriculum maps that can be designed by a participating school or district to highlight available units aligned with district or school curriculum frameworks.

High-level users have offered widely varying opinions of the UbD Exchange. Those with the most experience working with Understanding by Design tend to be the Exchange's strongest advocates. For example, Janie Smith, a UbD cadre member and a former curriculum developer from Alexandria, Virginia, states

> I use samples of units [from the UbD Exchange] in almost every workshop. In addition, in multiple-day workshops, I try to do a demonstration to show various uses. In three or more days with a group, I try to get them in a computer lab and have them enter units if they're a member of the [E]xchange or use the demo if they're not. I have also created my own unit on the [E]xchange.

Although high-level users commend the Exchange's usefulness as a tool for districtwide and school-level curriculum development, they tend to express some concern about its ease of access and current organization. For example, Corriero of New Jersey indicates that "some of our teachers have posted on the site and received feedback. In general, I would like to see more exemplary models posted so we can use them in reference to what the end product might look like, particularly in specific subject areas."

Overall, high-level users agree that the UbD Exchange has the potential to become a powerful resource, but recommend continuing modification of its organization. For example, Ken O'Connor, a UbD cadre member from Scarborough, Ontario, Canada, states, "I like the idea of the [E]xchange, but I think it needs to be organized so it is easier to access quality units and avoid incomplete and/or low-quality units."

Professional Development Online

In the autumn of 2002, ASCD launched three PD Online courses on Understanding by Design, each of which can be used to award approximately 21 Continuing Education Units to professionals seeking recertification.

These courses appear to have enormous potential for expanding the availability of training opportunities for a majority of staff members. This approach to professional development is a means to provide both follow-up for staff after the completion of an initial training cycle and initial training for staff members new to a school that has been working with UbD for an extended period.

Levine, Solovey, and Tatum of Tennessee describe the PD Online courses' value as a means to induct new teachers in the use of the framework: "We will use these [courses] as new teachers come on board during the summer of 2003. We are expecting an increase in enrollment next year. Therefore, additional teachers will be hired."

However, a majority of high-level users confess to having little if any direct experience with the actual courses or their application in their respective schools and districts. On the survey, their reactions and responses range from "No experience" and "We haven't tried them yet" to "We have read about them, but we haven't used them." Others

have expressed a certain reservation about the idea of electronic professional development. Meara of New Jersey, for example, declares:
"Hands-on, in-person [professional development is] always better."

■   ■   ■

As noted earlier in this chapter, Figure 5.1 summarizes the 10 basic
themes that emerge from high-level users' comments on the problems
of professional development efforts. The organizational assessment
matrix in Figure 5.2 summarizes this chapter's big ideas, listing indicators of understanding-based staff development that you can use to evaluate the current professional development programs and practices in
your school and district. Once again, the insights abstracted from the
experiences of high-level UbD users can be applied to virtually any
aspect of educational reform and school renewal.

5.1	**THE TOP 10 COMMON PROBLEMS IN UBD STAFF DEVELOPMENT**

1. *The Inoculation Delusion:* Presenting staff development at the beginning of the year and never revisiting it, thereby assuming that the first shot should take care of everything.

2. *The "Stand and Deliver" Pitfall:* Failing to model UbD strategies and processes for adult training participants, thus emphasizing content delivery, not deep conceptual understanding.

3. *The Outside Consultant Dependency Model:* Relying exclusively on external experts rather than building internal capacity, which shows an unwillingness or inability to form an internal UbD training cadre.

4. *The "Atoms, Not Molecules" Approach:* Failing to put UbD in context or to demonstrate its alignment with other district priorities and initiatives, with the result that UbD's principles and strategies seem isolated or unique.

5. *The "Program" Fallacy:* Presenting UbD as another program for which teachers are responsible, rather than as a universal framework and a language for articulating research-based best practices.

6. *The Isolationist Dilemma:* Emphasizing UbD elements in isolation, rather than in the context of an overall philosophy and approach to instructional design that promotes student understanding.

7. *"It's the Follow-Up, Stupid!" Oversight:* Omitting opportunities for staff to test UbD's key elements and to enlist peer support and coaching to help improve classroom instruction.

8. *Overlooking the Power of Peer Review:* Failing to model and integrate peer review into all professional development sessions, which results in a lack of user understanding about how to evaluate and modify unit designs.

Continued

| 5.1 | **THE TOP 10 COMMON PROBLEMS IN UBD**
STAFF DEVELOPMENT |

9. *Failing to Put the Action into Action Research:* Treating professional development exclusively as a training process without incorporating practices (i.e., study groups, inquiry teams, and action research cohorts) that have proven effective in sustaining change and promoting participant ownership.

10. *Forgetting the Clientele:* Overlooking the need to engage all stakeholders in professional development of UbD by providing training for only a limited number of teachers or by failing to engage and actively involve administrators.

5.2 | **PROFESSIONAL DEVELOPMENT THAT PROMOTES STAFF OWNERSHIP AND DEEP UNDERSTANDING**

To what extent does professional development in your school or district reflect each of the following indicators?

INDICATOR	NOT EVIDENT	SOMEWHAT EVIDENT	EVIDENT	HIGHLY EVIDENT
1. Professional development is ongoing and job embedded; it addresses the specific needs of participants.	☐	☐	☐	☐
2. Staff development emphasizes participant understanding, rather than just "knowing–doing."	☐	☐	☐	☐
3. Through initial training and appropriate follow-up, participants grow in their ability to use training knowledge and skills; they exhibit one or more of the facets of understanding in their professional practice.	☐	☐	☐	☐
4. Professional development programs and practices emphasize the need for a collaborative community of learning.	☐	☐	☐	☐
5. When new training content is introduced, a variety of study groups is the preferred mode of delivery.	☐	☐	☐	☐

5.2   PROFESSIONAL DEVELOPMENT THAT PROMOTES STAFF OWNERSHIP AND DEEP UNDERSTANDING

To what extent does professional development in your school or district reflect each of the following indicators?

INDICATOR	NOT EVIDENT	SOMEWHAT EVIDENT	EVIDENT	HIGHLY EVIDENT
6. Participants receive ongoing opportunities to engage in inquiry and exploration of training content and strategies.	☐	☐	☐	☐
7. Professional development generally culminates in some form of action research; it explores how the use of key training elements will affect student achievement.	☐	☐	☐	☐
8. We are able to determine the "value added" of our training and professional development, especially their effect on student achievement, staff performance, and organizational productivity.	☐	☐	☐	☐
9. Professional development is designed to help participants move along predictable stages of concern, from initial knowledge to ultimate internalization and independent application.	☐	☐	☐	☐

Continued

INDICATOR	NOT EVIDENT	SOMEWHAT EVIDENT	EVIDENT	HIGHLY EVIDENT
10. Through collaboration and ongoing program evaluation, we modify our professional development activities and practices to ensure maximum effect and participant understanding.	☐	☐	☐	☐

6

IMPROVING PRESERVICE
TRAINING AND TEACHER-
INDUCTION PROGRAMS

ESSENTIAL QUESTIONS

1. *How can Understanding by Design help new educators promote understanding, not just knowledge–recall, among their students?*

2. *What are the lessons learned about the relationship between Understanding by Design and preservice teacher preparation?*

3. *How can educators integrate Understanding by Design into the design and implementation of meaningful preservice and teacher-induction programs?*

A critical issue facing school districts today involves the preparation of teachers in preservice situations for success with diverse student populations. In light of the growing numbers of Baby Boomer retirees and the high level of teacher turnover in many regions, districts must face a double-edged sword: replacing growing numbers of teachers while confronting critics who demand more rigorous accountability and higher student achievement of increasingly ambitious standards.

This chapter accents ways in which Understanding by Design can complement preservice and teacher-induction experiences in a variety of settings. Experienced users of UbD share insights and recommend ways to help teachers-in-training or newly hired teachers grow in their understanding and use of research-based best practices, particularly in the areas of designing effective learner outcomes, assessing and evaluating student understanding, and teaching for understanding. High-level users also shed light on the role of the mentoring process in new teacher induction, including what it takes for a new hire to understand district requirements and policies, sustain a positive attitude, work well with a variety of students, and internalize the implications of curriculum guides and frameworks to promote student understanding and achievement. The final section uses the six facets of understanding (explanation, interpretation, application, perspective, empathy, and self-knowledge) to frame all aspects of the mentoring and peer coaching processes.

An Overview: UbD and New Teacher Preparation

Survey participants, focus group members, and interview subjects have indicated the following about the relationship between and among UbD, induction programs for new teachers, and related forms of cross-institutional partnerships involving teacher preparation:

• In many regions, new educators appear to have received some direct training in research-based best practices consistent with UbD's tenets, including cognitive learning theory, constructivist teaching principles, brain-compatible teaching and learning, and multiple intelligences and learning styles.

• Despite growing evidence of preservice training that addresses such issues, many new teachers seem overwhelmed by the requirements and expectations of their profession, especially those teachers who are noncertified or are in the process of a career transition.

• New teachers' anxiety is compounded by several issues that are almost universal throughout the profession today, including the challenge of classroom management and the need to prepare students for high-stakes accountability testing.

- Most new teachers have received training in lesson plan design and development, but many have little, if any, experience in unit design, especially long-term planning over the course of an academic year.

- Although new teachers have some familiarity with contemporary instructional strategies, they need much more professional development in promoting mastery of standards among diverse student populations while using a range of assessment tools and differentiated instruction.

- The most effective programs for teacher preparation and induction have a cross-institutional design that includes mentoring opportunities for new hires and meaningful professional development for both mentors and mentees.

Preservice Training Programs and the Emerging Needs of New Teachers: Where Are We Now?

In light of the growing need for qualified teachers during a time of massive turnover, what do the comments of Understanding by Design practitioners suggest about the state of preservice training programs at colleges and universities? Perhaps predictably, the answer is mixed. Many participants affirm that they are beginning to see evidence that those institutions now pay more attention to research-based best practices. At the same time, they acknowledge that newly hired teachers share many of the same issues and concerns, including how to acclimate themselves to the culture of teaching, manage their classrooms successfully, and deal with the increasingly diverse needs of their students.

High-level users also assert that schools rarely view UbD as an immediate priority for new teachers. For example, Frank Champine, a social studies lead teacher in K–12 at the Neshaminy School District, Department of Curriculum and Instruction, Langhorne, Pennsylvania, states, "We focus our new teachers on survival skills first. Essential elements of instruction and classroom management [are the main emphases] in our induction program. UbD is reserved for the more experienced teacher at this time." Similarly, Elliott Seif, a UbD cadre member from Philadelphia and a former curriculum and staff development director in Bucks County, Pennsylvania, describes "limited integration. . . . Most districts feel that new teachers have enough on their plate without complicating their lives with UbD. Usually [the districts] wait until the second or third year to introduce UbD."

According to high-level users, newly hired teachers generally need specific support in the following areas:

- Understanding rules, procedures, and school operations.

- Dealing with issues of classroom management and discipline.

- Learning to deal with the range of student needs, including issues related to special populations, such as gifted and talented, special education, ESL, and socioeconomically disadvantaged students.

- Adapting to the norms and mores of the school as a learning organization, including finding their own path and connection to the school's social order, subgroups, and administrative expectations.

- Overcoming a sense of isolation and anxiety that arises within any new profession, but especially one as challenging as contemporary education.

The good news is that there seems to be a growing recognition of the need to incorporate frameworks like UbD into both preservice and teacher-induction programs. Judith Hilton, a UbD cadre member and university professor from Greenwood Village, Colorado, describes one such initiative:

I coordinate the college curriculum for an alternative licensure program in Colorado that has brought over 600 people into education who hold degrees but no license to teach. We use UbD for their Teacher Work Sample (a comprehensive unit of study required for licensure). I trained the cohort instructors. They teach the candidates; [candidates] are evaluated by their building administrator [and are] supported by a building mentor, the cohort instructors, and a coach through a United States Department of Education grant. Our results show that these teachers are as good as or better than those trained traditionally. The retention is better, the program has more teachers of color, and we're gathering data about student performance. Most of the teachers are placed in unsatisfactory or poorly performing inner-city schools, so again, using Colorado state tests where there is poverty, [high enrollment in] ESL, high mobility, and other uncontrollable variables makes it a challenge, but we must be doing something right because we have secured an additional $2 million in funding.

When reflecting on the universal needs of individuals entering the teaching profession, high-level users generally recommend incorporating the following UbD principles and strategies into the process of new teacher training and orientation:

1. Introduce the concept of unpacking standards—including use of the three-circle curriculum audit to determine (a) what is worth being familiar with, (b) what all students should know and be able to do, and (c) what all students should understand—as part of both preservice and induction training for new teachers.

2. Stress the importance of using cueing devices to help students understand the purpose of what they are studying and the big ideas that unify the smaller curricular elements. Preservice and new teacher trainees can benefit from involvement in developing and using the essential questions and enduring understandings.

3. Help preservice and newly hired teachers to understand how they can address and monitor students' growing understanding as they

use the six facets of understanding: explanation, interpretation, application, perspective, empathy, and self-knowledge.

4. Emphasize the need for a balanced and complete assessment process in all teachers' classrooms, including use of a photo album of assessment data derived from tests and quizzes with constructed-response items; reflective assessments (logs, journals, peer response groups); academic prompts; and the students' culminating performance tasks and projects.

5. Stress using the elements of WHERETO (see Chapter 1, page 19) as guidelines for designing lessons and units, and emphasize the value of putting the learner at the center of the learning process through carefully designed instructional activities.

Teacher-Induction Programs and Understanding by Design

To address the previously identified problems, many districts are now incorporating UbD—or at least certain of its principles and strategies—as part of their efforts to help new hires become successful. For example, Joseph Corriero, assistant superintendent for curriculum and instruction in Cranford, New Jersey, asserts, "All new teachers are exposed to UbD as part of the New Teacher Orientation Program. They also see it in their curriculum guides." Similarly, Tony Spears, director of curriculum and professional development in the San Diego County Office of Education, San Diego, California, states, "Our county's Beginning Teacher Support Assessment (BTSA) program has used the [UbD] process in its classroom observations, lesson study, and professional development."

Like all high-level users who identify UbD as an essential element of their teacher-induction programs, Lynne Meara, supervisor of instruction and gifted and talented coordinator for the Plumsted Township School District in New Egypt, New Jersey, emphasizes the need for long-term, rather than quick-fix, approaches to staff development for new hires:

> Our nontenured teachers receive a three-day staff development and inservice [training session] during the summer. Our first-year teachers receive a traditional welcome to the district, complete with support and mentoring. Our second- and third-year teachers will have development sessions in both UbD and lesson study from both teacher facilitators and our own curriculum staff development team. This will give them the time and opportunity to learn about the processes and develop some lessons using the format. Although the framework is new to them, they have already been introduced to the language during their observations and conferences.

Jill Levine, Judy Solovey, and Joyce Tatum of the Normal Park Museum Magnet School in Chattanooga, Tennessee, reinforce the contention of many high-level users that new teachers need professional development in formal unit design: "New teachers will receive two days of UbD training and will work with grade-level colleagues to refine and develop current units. Each grade teaches between four and six UbD units each year."

This component of teacher-induction programs reflects high-level users' universal perception that new teachers need much more support and assistance as they design instructional tasks and teach episodes. Specifically, high-level users recommend that the teacher-induction process incorporate the following key themes:

• *The need to understand and apply research-based best practices and the learning theory underlying those practices.* Professional development in teacher-induction programs should include sustained emphasis on the best of what we know about teaching and learning, particularly when promoting student understanding, not just knowledge–recall. UbD reflects current theory and research related to cognitive learning theory, constructivist teaching principles, brain-compatible teaching and learning, the power of cueing tools and advance organizers, and the value of putting the learner first.

• *The need to plan for long-term, not short-term, desired results.* New teachers can benefit enormously from UbD's emphasis on backward design and its contention that effective teaching and learning begins with the end in mind. Professional development programs, therefore, should help new teachers understand what standards they must teach and how to unpack those standards. This process should include sustained work to determine which aspects of a standard require deep conceptual understanding on the part of students and which elements can be taught at the knowledge–skill level of competence.

• *The relationship between and among desired results, assessment, and instruction.* New teachers require support to understand that curriculum is a management system to monitor and reinforce learning for all students. Teacher-induction programs, therefore, should support new hires in addressing the deep connection among the identified learner outcomes, the process of assessing learner progress in achieving those outcomes, and the power of teaching for understanding.

• *The value of collaboration via lesson and unit study.* New teachers should participate in regular lesson and unit design activities designed to help them critique their own lessons and units, as well as those of their peers. Through the process of peer review and study group discussion, new teachers can grow to understand and apply effective instructional design practices focused on long-term, rather than "seat-of-the-pants," lesson planning.

• *The need to differentiate instruction to accommodate all students' strengths and needs.* While addressing the needs of diverse student populations, newly hired teachers can benefit from investigating UbD's approach to design and implementation. All students, for example, need to understand where they are going, how they will get there, and how they will be evaluated along the way. Engaged and enthused learners need a clear sense of the connection between themselves and the content they are studying. Experience-based and inquiry-oriented learning that centers the student in the learning process is much more effective than didactic, teacher-talk behavior. Similarly, the learner must play an active role in self-regulation and self-evaluation. Finally, teachers must monitor student achievement and adjust their teaching to address both individual and small-group needs. They must ensure that all learners move toward independent use of knowledge and skills, as well as increase deep conceptual understanding of the curriculum.

Characteristics of Effective Cross-Institutional Educational Partnerships and Mentoring Programs

Finally, high-level users acknowledge the value and power of cross-institutional partnerships involving college, university, and community partners working closely with schools and districts to help all students succeed. For instance, Margaret Searle, an educational consultant in Perrysburg, Ohio, describes the effect of such collaborations, particularly when they emphasize the mentoring process:

> The state-level training allows districts to send teams of six [people] to a central training [session]. These teams are to include new teachers, special and regular education, as well as one administrator. This becomes the leadership team to go back and implement at least a part of what they have learned.

Angela Ryan, an instructional facilitator in Hershey, Pennsylvania, describes her district's teacher-induction program and how it reflects UbD:

> Beginning this August 2003, I will be leading a three-day training [workshop] for all new teachers. This is mandated for new teachers and takes the place of a standards-driven unit workshop previously required. All units that these teachers write will be UbD based. Over time, [as new teachers continue to join our district and attend this

workshop,] we will build UbD-written curriculum, as well as consistency among the faculty. Penn State University, College of Education, has adopted UbD as a major emphasis for curriculum design. Because of a special partnership our school has with Penn State University, all student teachers—and specifically those coming to our school—have UbD training. Part of the Penn State requirement is a UbD-based unit. I help facilitate this with our student teachers.

Although high-level users have varied experiences with such cross-institutional partnerships, all acknowledge the potential value of and need for such collaborations. At the same time, however, many point to the following challenges and barriers that school and district staffs must address when setting up such partnerships:

• The proliferation of needs among many schools and districts necessitates that participating organizations have a clear sense of the scope and potential limitations of what a cross-institutional partnership can accomplish.

• The very real issue of limited resources, both in terms of funding and personnel, frequently results in partnerships becoming a series of meetings between participating organizations with little sustained follow-through or concrete accomplishments. When those organizations and schools or districts are stretched thin, there is a potential for cross-institutional collaborations to become public relations activities, rather than a means to change organizational practices and to increase accomplishments.

• A potential exists for organizational culture clashes that result from differing organizational norms, standards, and practices. Schools frequently operate on time lines and deadlines that are more accelerated than those of most colleges and universities and less accelerated than those of most business partners.

• The complexity of determining desired results for cross-institutional partnerships can cause education staffs to emphasize high-stakes accountability test results. Likewise, the university and business partners can struggle to understand how they can directly contribute to improving test scores.

- A struggle can emerge while assessing how much value cross-institutional partnerships really add, especially when participating organizations have widely differing ways of evaluating progress and determining benchmarks. It is one thing to encourage cross-institutional communication and collaboration; it is quite another to confirm how such activities produce tangible, empirical results.

Because of these potential barriers and the very real problems that new teachers face when entering the profession, the value and significance of mentors emerges as a major recurrent theme among survey participants' discussion of Understanding by Design and how they use UbD in their respective schools and districts. As Searle of Ohio reports, "[As a result of our program], new teachers are always coming up and saying, 'Thank God! Now I know what to do and who can help me.'"

The long-range teacher-induction program that she describes, like programs of many high-level users, ensures that teachers receive one-on-one support from at least one mentor during their first three years of teaching.

Effective mentoring programs inherently reflect both the UbD principle of a learner at the center of the learning process and the support provided by a teacher who functions as a coach and critical friend. As new teachers learn, especially during their initial three years, they should think about the range and complexity of what they must know, do, and understand, including

- Requirements of the curricula they are to teach, including standards, objectives, performance indicators, assessment requirements, and instructional implications.

• Backgrounds, strengths, and needs of specific students, as well as the overall student population served by their school.

• Policies, procedures, and practices of both the school and district of which they are now a part.

• Tools and strategies for classroom management, including ways to make the learning process both relevant and meaningful to all learners.

• Standards for which they are accountable, including the professional standard on which they will be evaluated and the curriculum standards that they are expected to have all their students master.

The mentoring programs that high-level users describe generally reflect the research-based best practices common to effective programs with sustained track records, as well as UbD design principles. General practices include, but are not limited to, the following:

• Assigning a mentor with demonstrated success as a teacher and with a proven understanding of the content.

• Articulating clear expectations about the mentor's role, including providing counsel and coaching related to classroom management, school policies and practices, and methods for dealing with curriculum and instructional design and delivery.

• Recognizing that the mentor should serve as a coach and confidant, not as an evaluator.

• Setting aside a reasonable amount of time to ensure that mentor and mentee can meet regularly without undue constraints or impositions on other professional duties.

• Assessing the mentoring programs' benefits in terms of teacher retention rates and in degrees of professional success and job satisfaction.

High-level users recommend the following UbD principles as appropriate tenets for effective mentoring programs, including programs that involve cross-institutional partnerships:

• *Begin with the end in mind to establish a core curriculum.* Like effective teaching and learning practices, productive mentoring programs require that the mentor and mentee, as well as the organizations they represent, be clear about desired results. What, for example, will determine whether mentoring is successful for both partners? What should the mentor help the mentee become familiar with? What should the mentee know and be able to do more effectively as a result of mentoring? What should both partners understand at a deeper level because of their collaboration and shared inquiry?

• *Achieve consensus about professional standards.* As part of beginning with the end in mind, both mentor and mentee must be partners in unpacking and addressing the professional competencies for which the mentee is responsible. Through a shared analysis in which the partners explore the mentee's status at the beginning of the relationship and how mentoring can help improve the mentee's performance, the partners can direct their efforts to ensure the mentee's professional success.

• *Use the six facets of understanding to guide the mentee's growth and professional proficiency.* Just as a teacher can use the facets to determine learning objectives and accompanying assessments, the mentor and mentee can use them to monitor their progress together. For example, how does mentoring help the new teacher become more adept at explaining and applying research-based best practices in assessment and instruction? How is the mentee improving in interpreting student behaviors that require intervention, coaching, or disciplinary measures? To what extent has mentoring helped the new teacher analyze varying perspectives expressed by students? Has the mentee's empathy for all learners—particularly those who present problems and challenges—increased as a result of mentoring? Finally, how has mentoring contributed to the mentee's capacity for self-knowledge as reflected in enhanced levels of self-assessment, self-regulation, and spontaneous ability to reflect, revisit, revise, and rethink practices and attitudes?

- *Incorporate a genuine photo album approach to assessing and evaluating the mentoring partnership and its effect on the mentee's professional performance.* Like good teaching, good mentoring encourages educators to use a range of assessment tools. The mentoring partnership should include opportunities for self-reflection and self-assessment on both partners' parts. It should also include a range of performance tasks—from a focus on lesson and unit design to cognitive coaching in the classroom—that can become benchmarks to monitor and evaluate progress. Coaching can range from a mentor scripting a lesson, to co-teaching a lesson or lesson segment, to helping the mentee understand and implement new instructional practices and strategies.

- *Apply what works in the classroom to promote the success of the mentee.* Once again, WHERETO (see Chapter 1, page 19) can be extraordinarily useful in guiding and shaping discussions and coaching activities involving a mentor and mentee. Through natural observation, mentor feedback, and mentee self-reflection, the mentoring partnership can enhance mentees' understanding of *where* they are going, *why* they are going there, and *ways* in which they will be evaluated in their professional setting (the "W" element). Mentoring can enrich mentees' sense of personal and professional efficacy, "hooking" their interest in and commitment to the teaching process (the "H" element). It can also *equip* mentees for success by fostering inquiry-driven analysis of their experiences within the classroom and ways to sustain their professional growth and commitment (the first "E" element). A successful mentor-mentee relationship has enormous potential for helping new teachers *reflect, revisit, revise,* and *rethink* (the "R" element) their attitudes, instructional practices, and relationships with their students. The process of mentoring can also expand mentees' ability to *self-evaluate* and to express or *exhibit* their growing professional knowledge, skills, and understandings (the second "E" element). Successful mentoring allows participants to *tailor* (the "T" element) professional development and coaching opportunities in order to maximize their potential as an educator. Finally, mentors can help mentees move from basic teaching knowledge and skills to increasing levels of conceptual understanding and independent application (the "O" element).

■   ■   ■

Although this study finds that UbD-based cross-institutional partnerships are in their infant stages in many schools and districts, they have nonetheless proven extremely successful in promoting professional expertise and understanding. Mentoring has especially striking and powerful implications for improving the professional expertise of new teachers, as well as for providing a genuine opportunity for growth and enrichment for the seasoned professional. As you consider the role of teacher-preparation programs in your own school, district, or related learning organization, you may wish to use Figure 6.1 to begin or enrich professional dialogue. In addition, Figure 6.2 summarizes key elements of effective mentoring programs that reflect UbD's principles and big ideas.

6.1 | PRESERVICE AND TEACHER-INDUCTION PROGRAMS THAT PROMOTE NEW TEACHER SUCCESS

To what extent do preservice and teacher-induction programs in your school or district reflect each of the following indicators?

INDICATOR	NOT EVIDENT	SOMEWHAT EVIDENT	EVIDENT	HIGHLY EVIDENT
1. We encourage cross-institutional partnerships designed to ensure that teachers enter our school or district prepared for success.	☐	☐	☐	☐
2. Our partnerships reinforce consensus-driven desired results for teacher professionalism and teacher retention.	☐	☐	☐	☐
3. Our cross-institutional partnerships reinforce our commitment to ensuring that all students achieve a deep conceptual understanding of our standards as a result of teachers who deeply understand what they teach.	☐	☐	☐	☐
4. As part of our cross-institutional partnerships, we have a comprehensive evaluation plan that monitors and evaluates the degree of success and the retention of our newly hired staff.	☐	☐	☐	☐

6.1 | PRESERVICE AND TEACHER-INDUCTION PROGRAMS THAT PROMOTE NEW TEACHER SUCCESS

To what extent do preservice and teacher-induction programs in your school or district reflect each of the following indicators?

INDICATOR	NOT EVIDENT	SOMEWHAT EVIDENT	EVIDENT	HIGHLY EVIDENT
5. Our evaluation plan allows us to determine the value each partnership adds, including how each affects student achievement, staff productivity, and organizational effectiveness.	☐	☐	☐	☐
6. We incorporate a variety of formative and summative evaluation processes, thus generating a professional portfolio of our accomplishments in partnerships.	☐	☐	☐	☐
7. Our cross-institutional partnerships include active outreach to colleges and universities involved in preservice training programs.	☐	☐	☐	☐
8. As a result of our partnerships with college and university preservice training programs, new teachers have a clear understanding of our expectations for lesson and unit design, classroom management, assessment and evaluation, and instructional delivery.	☐	☐	☐	☐

Continued

INDICATOR	NOT EVIDENT	SOMEWHAT EVIDENT	EVIDENT	HIGHLY EVIDENT
9. Our teacher-induction program allows new hires to understand our school's or district's expectations and operations while effectively ensuring that all students are equipped for success.	☐	☐	☐	☐
10. Our teacher-induction program represents a multiyear commitment to ensure that new teachers receive the support and resources required for success.	☐	☐	☐	☐

6.2 | MENTORING PROGRAMS THAT PROMOTE NEW TEACHER SUCCESS

To what extent do mentoring programs in your school or district reflect each of the following indicators?

INDICATOR	NOT EVIDENT	SOMEWHAT EVIDENT	EVIDENT	HIGHLY EVIDENT
1. We offer a variety of multi-year mentoring programs designed to help new teachers succeed.	☐	☐	☐	☐
2. Our mentoring programs help new teachers understand their roles and responsibilities.	☐	☐	☐	☐
3. Our mentoring programs help new teachers successfully address the professional standards for which they are accountable.	☐	☐	☐	☐
4. Our mentoring programs help new teachers acquire and apply strategies, practices, and habits of mind they need to be successful and achieve identified professional standards.	☐	☐	☐	☐
5. Our mentoring programs help new teachers use classroom management techniques and strategies that promote success for students of varying needs and from diverse populations.	☐	☐	☐	☐

Continued

INDICATOR	NOT EVIDENT	SOMEWHAT EVIDENT	EVIDENT	HIGHLY EVIDENT
6. Our mentoring programs help new teachers implement research-based practices for instructional design and delivery.	☐	☐	☐	☐
7. Our mentoring programs help new teachers understand the range of human and material resources available to ensure their sense of efficacy and job satisfaction.	☐	☐	☐	☐
8. Our mentoring programs have clearly articulated desired results for all participants, both mentors and mentees.	☐	☐	☐	☐
9. We use a range of assessment tools and processes to collect and analyze formative and summative evaluation data to determine the value added and effect of our mentoring programs relative to desired results.	☐	☐	☐	☐
10. Our mentoring programs concentrate on research-based coaching, intervention, and related support strategies.	☐	☐	☐	☐

FACILITATING ORGANIZATION DEVELOPMENT, CONTINUOUS IMPROVEMENT, AND STRATEGIC PLANNING

ESSENTIAL QUESTIONS

1. *How can Understanding by Design expand beyond unit development to become a catalyst for organizational renewal?*

2. *What have experienced users of Understanding by Design learned about changing organizational norms and cultures?*

3. *How can Understanding by Design complement the strategic planning and continuous improvement processes in educational organizations?*

4. *What is needed to determine the value that Understanding by Design adds, including design recommendations for potential program evaluation studies?*

A significant and logical extension of any discussion of professional development is the issue of transforming educational organizations into communities of learning. As stressed in Lieberman and Miller (1999) and in Joyce, Wolf, and Calhoun (1993), real transformation of teaching and learning requires that stakeholders remain lifelong learners who work together to solve problems, make decisions, and ensure long-term productivity. Perhaps most significantly, a viable community of inquiry and learning centers itself on the principle of continuous improvement. This process involves a clear articulation of desired results for the organization, purposeful data collection and analysis; and consequent adjustment of policies, practices, and procedures. All should be based on long-term action planning.

High-level users of Understanding by Design (UbD) frequently cite the very real and obvious parallels between this philosophy of long-range strategic planning and the tenets of the UbD framework. They assert that UbD—especially its backward design process—can serve as a vehicle to promote and sustain active learning communities that are dedicated to teaching for understanding, rather than teaching students simply to repeat or mimic key knowledge and skills. This chapter extends our UbD investigation to the area of improving organizational cultures through strategic planning. Every district has some protocol for school improvement planning. Frequently, however, this process is characterized by a top-down or committee-mandated plan that most stakeholders either misunderstand or disregard.

This chapter examines what UbD implies for successful team building and institutional renorming through organizational development. How, for example, can we shift toward a collaborative work culture in which all stakeholders play an active role in understanding and supporting the site's strategic planning process? How can we work together to ensure success for all? Finally, how can we overcome inevitable resistance to change associated with adopting and implementing UbD?

Understanding by Design at the System Level: Practitioner Reflections

High-level users express varying opinions of how the various aspects of UbD can serve as a catalyst for system change. Generally, however, most agree on four ways that the backward design process might be applied for organizational improvement: (1) as a vehicle for transforming curriculum and instruction, (2) as a unifying influence for professional development, (3) as a framework for guiding and informing long-range planning, and (4) as a common language and philosophical context for shaping organizational improvement.

Joseph Corriero, assistant superintendent for curriculum and instruction in Cranford, New Jersey, emphasizes that "[UbD] has become accepted as the preferred teaching–learning model in the district. It is incorporated into our long-range plan, as well as yearly goals. It is the core of our professional development planning."

Similarly, Lynne Meara, supervisor of instruction and gifted and talented coordinator for the Plumsted Township School District in New Egypt, New Jersey, describes the relationship between UbD and strategic planning for curriculum: "Our seven-year curriculum development plan is directly tied to the UbD process and, in the future, will become part of the action research component of our differentiated supervision model."

Deborah Jo Alberti, assistant director for special and gifted education services in the Norfolk Public Schools, Norfolk, Virginia, asserts that

> Prior to our work with UbD, our school division had not articulated a philosophy of teaching and learning; we now have one completely based on research and posted throughout the school division. Our philosophy of learning and our commitment to "powerful literacy" are, in my opinion, a direct result of our work with UbD. Working with UbD principles cannot help but make one push the envelope, [due to the framework's] basis in rigor and challenge, thinking and reasoning.

Similarly, Alberti identifies powerful connections between her district's professional development initiatives and UbD:

The importance of staff development in many other areas became very evident when we began our work with UbD because UbD raised the bar for us in terms of our understanding of pedagogy, assessment, teaching, and learning. For me, it was one of the few "tools" that had accomplished this and forced us to look differently at what was really important and whether we were organized to support and sustain such work. Our new Department of Leadership and Capacity Development surfaced in response [to the need] to have a more effective system of increasing our professional staff's capacity to meet higher standards.

Mark Wise, a social studies supervisor at Grover Middle School in Princeton Junction, New Jersey, emphasizes the unifying power of UbD within the process of strategic planning and continuous improvement:

We, as a middle school administrative team, have begun to develop our long-term planning using backward design as a model. The most recent example is how we developed and implemented our schedule change. We first thought about both product and process with the end in mind, and then we backed into how we would get there. We developed our guiding principles for what a middle school should look like and developed student competencies for what they should know and be able to do upon graduation, and then [we] began to draft potential schedules.

Alyce Anderson, principal of the Herbertsville Elementary School in Brick, New Jersey, confirms the potential of UbD as a catalyst for transforming school cultures:

[UbD] promotes collegiality; [it] currently [is] used as a vehicle for action research and the peer review process [and is] utilized as a framework to structure committee agendas. The School-Based Objectives action plan includes elements of UbD, and [the UbD] framework promotes continuous improvement through focus on the teacher as researcher.

Understanding by Design and the Continuous Improvement Process

High-level users have identified the following big ideas concerning connections between the UbD framework and the processes of continuous improvement, strategic planning, and organization development:

• Investigate and articulate what stakeholders believe to be the big ideas and essential questions for which a school, district, or other learning organization is responsible.

• Use enduring understandings and essential questions to revise and reframe existing vision and mission statements.

• Use a consensus-driven set of understandings, questions, and reframed vision and mission statements to determine measurable long-range goals, performance indicators, and time lines for achieving goals in relation to both accountability standards and identified gaps in student achievement.

• Use the processes of continuous improvement and strategic planning as vehicles for ensuring that all students achieve success, particularly in understanding what they are learning. These processes should consistently use data disaggregation to examine how subgroups of students are performing and improving relative to identified targets.

• Consider how the six facets of understanding can become guidelines and framing tools for addressing student understanding. This process can include an analysis of standardized test designs and areas in which students are underperforming because they lack deep understanding.

• Use a variety of assessment and evaluation tools (in addition to required standardized tests) to monitor students' continuous improvement. As UbD advocates, include reflections, academic prompts, and culminating performance tasks and projects.

• Use this photo album of assessment and evaluation tools to create a school portfolio that reflects the range of staff and student achievements relative to identified targets. Use the tools to confirm staff conclusions and insights about organizational progress.

• Provide meaningful and ongoing professional development to ensure that all staff members own the process of continuous improvement.

• Modify and adjust the school improvement plan as new data become available, emphasizing how various programs, frameworks, and strategies—identified as plan interventions—actually add value.

• Communicate to all stakeholders the organization's performance outcomes, and enlist stakeholder support in promoting continuous improvement.

Schools can benefit from exploring key UbD principles as guidelines for continuous improvement. Figure 7.1, at the end of this chapter, identifies behaviors associated with learning organizations that promote all students' understanding. This diagram provides recommended long-range goals for strategic planning and the parallel UbD principles that support goal achievement.

A New Paradigm for Instructional Leadership

According to high-level users, integrating UbD into a school's or a district's continuous improvement requires a shared commitment to the idea of instructional leadership. Virtually every respondent acknowledges that if school and district leaders are not active participants in and supporters of the UbD framework, it becomes, in essence, another flavor of the month. Perhaps most important, high-level users concede that when administrators do not complete actual UbD units themselves, they have little, if any, deep understanding of what they must do to support teacher use of UbD.

Overall, high-level users also express commitment to the value of collaboration and shared governance. Instructional leadership, they contend, must involve all major stakeholders, with an emphasis on teacher leadership, while working with and implementing UbD and related changes. Expert practitioners' recommendations for ensuring effective leadership within the learning organization have centered on the following key themes:

• *The need for a shared vision, mission, and commitment to integrate UbD into overall school improvement efforts.* An effective instructional leader, particularly the principal, must work closely with all stakeholders to plan for UbD implementation. Leaders must ensure that all UbD participants understand and address the research base, purposes, and proposed long-range goals. This emerging collaborative commitment must clearly align with student achievement goals and staff efforts to promote goal attainment.

• *The need to set aside time and resources to support the institutionalization of UbD.* No more significant responsibility exists for instructional leaders than providing the time, training, and related human and material resources to help all staff members acquire and integrate the components of a new professional development initiative. For example, high-level users stress that educators need time to discuss and internalize new strategies and practices. They must have appropriate coaching and support, including peer review opportunities, to internalize the UbD framework and to work through any areas of confusion or dissonance. Effective leaders promote staff commitment to the long term, not the short term, and avoid any appearance or perception of UbD as a quick fix or magic bullet.

• *The need to empower staff and "build" school-based trainers and leaders to create a culture of collaboration with clearly articulated roles and responsibilities.* Although high-level users generally acknowledge the almost inevitable emergence of early UbD adopters and pioneers, educators who resist change must receive support and leadership to ensure their buy-in. Effective instructional leaders work with staff to identify and implement clearly articulated UbD roles and responsibilities as well as to show UbD's connections to overall efforts to improve student achievement, staff productivity, and organizational effectiveness.

• *The power of promoting alignment to overcome organizational, program, and staff isolation.* A major recurrent idea expressed by most high-level users is the need to overcome a sense of separation and isolation that pervades many educational organizations. Effective instructional leaders, therefore, work with staff members to overcome isolation factors such as a lack of communication and articulation across grade levels and content areas. In a district implementing UbD, it is especially critical for leaders to promote cross-school and cross-level discussions that will help elementary, middle, and high school educators understand one another's programs, curricula, and accountability responsibilities. Once again, high-level users advocate a one-for-all approach to instructional leadership. They also stress that effective leaders are collaborators rather than traditional managers and assert that organizational change and renewal are everyone's responsibility.

• *The need for consensus-building and shared construction of meaning.* A variation of the previous theme is high-level users' consistent affirmation of the power surrounding collaboration and staff construction of meaning about UbD and its implications for change and renewal. UbD users return many times to the idea that all staff members must receive training, support, and coaching to build a shared consensus about (1) what the UbD framework means; (2) how it can best be implemented; and (3) what its unique implications are for their individual, content, and grade-level issues and responsibilities. Participants also reiterate the need for instructional leaders to model and integrate UbD principles into all facets of professional development (i.e., a clear set of outcomes that emphasize staff understanding, a strategic plan to assess and evaluate training results, and a set of training activities aligned with the WHERETO principles).

The Program Evaluation Process: Implications for Continuous Improvement

As we stress in earlier sections of this book, high-level users unanimously affirm the need for long-term evaluation evidence for UbD. Their conviction centers on the essential issue involving strategic planning and continuous improvement today: the accountability movement and accompanying pressures on educators to confirm how interventions and instructional programs affect achievement.

Experienced UbD practitioners recurrently and consistently cite the following concerns about meaningful program evaluation and related performance data:

• No Child Left Behind federal mandates require educational organizations to demonstrate a solid research base that includes educational frameworks, programs, and strategies in grant applications and in program development initiatives that are federally funded.

• State-level economic factors (including growing state deficits) necessitate triage regarding what stays and what goes in professional development, curriculum design, assessment, and related areas.

• A growing trend in many districts is to confirm the value-added aspects of frameworks, programs, and strategies that are used systemically.

• Increasing pressure exists to ensure that schools and districts use replicable frameworks and programs that are confirmed to make a difference in student achievement.

• National-, state-, district-, and school-level concerns abound regarding the search for frameworks and programs that have been proven effective among increasingly diverse special populations (e.g., gifted and talented, special education, ESL, and socioeconomically disadvantaged students).

• An increase in cross-institutional collaborations involves colleges and universities with school districts that are committed to addressing the teacher shortage and related certification issues by using preservice and teacher-induction programs grounded in research-based best practices.

In light of these issues, high-level users have identified the following research questions for long-term program evaluation studies of Understanding by Design:

1. How do we determine the level of UbD implementation at district and school levels?

2. How do we determine the value that UbD use adds to a school or district? For example, how can we determine correlations between high levels of UbD implementation and gains in standardized student achievement data?

3. How does UbD implementation affect the longitudinal progress of students in special populations?

4. How can we determine the effect of UbD use on school- and district-level organizational practices (e.g., curriculum design, development, and implementation; improvement in assessment practices; professional development practices; and instructional delivery)?

5. How can we determine the organizational norms and practices associated with successful UbD implementation at the school and district level, including, for example, leadership styles, practitioner research and study group activities, and curriculum modifications?

6. How can we replicate successful UbD strategies and program designs across all sites?

As schools and districts explore these issues, they must also confront the national imperative to use some variation of experimental research and evaluation processes to answer these questions. Accordingly, high-level users recommend that future evaluative studies of UbD investigate the following research hypotheses:

• There is a positive correlation between high levels of UbD implementation within a school and the students' longitudinal achievements, as measured by standardized tests and related district accountability measures.

• There are identifiable recurrent patterns of organizational practice and cultural norms (e.g., instructional leadership behaviors, curriculum design and implementation practices, assessment protocols, professional development criteria) associated with successful UbD implementation at a specific school or within a district.

• Capacity building for successful UbD implementation requires a commitment to data-driven continuous improvement, with modifications and enhancements of both school- and district-level practices and procedures related to curriculum, assessment, instruction, and professional development.

If we examine the responses of high-level users, potential organizing methodologies and focus areas for evaluation studies of UbD and its effect on student achievement, staff performance, and organizational productivity begin to emerge. Generally, high-level users suggest three approaches:

1. *Levels-of-implementation studies.* This type of study can determine the extent to which staff members have adopted and internalized Understanding by Design. After establishing baseline data, evaluators monitor growing levels of UbD use over time, employing variations of the Concerns-Based Adoption Model (CBAM) to determine where staff members are in relation to levels of adoption, internalization, and

use. (For example, Level 1 would indicate initial knowledge acquisition; Level 2 would indicate evidence of some classroom use; Level 3 would indicate continuing and expanding UbD use by a system or school cadre, with emergent use among most other educators; Level 4 would indicate evidence of substantive organizational change; and Level 5 would indicate operationalized UbD as part of the overall school culture.)

2. *Context and value-added evaluation studies.* This kind of study can assess UbD's effect on practitioners' behaviors, attitudes, and practices, and thus emphasize how UbD has contributed to student achievement, staff productivity, and organizational effectiveness. It provides the means of quantifying the organizational effect of UbD implementation, including discernible changes in organizational norms and culture, as well as in policies and practices related to curriculum, assessment, instruction, professional development, and instructional leadership. In the value-added approach, evaluators establish baseline student performance data about standardized accountability measures and longitudinal analysis of correlations between growing UbD use and changes in student achievement data.

3. *Randomly controlled experimental studies.* This is the most formal and, perhaps, the most ambitious of the three recommended approaches. Called the "gold standard approach" by Robert Slavin (1983) of Johns Hopkins University, it involves studying experimental and control groups to evaluate the empirically verifiable correlations between high levels of UbD use and student achievement levels on high-stakes accountability tests. Participating educators receive a comprehensive training program to confirm their qualification as high-level users (with triangulation through teacher observations using a validated observation checklist and protocol). Over a multiyear period, evaluators would compare student achievement results on standardized accountability measures for the experimental group against student achievement results of randomly selected educators who are teaching the same subjects but without UbD training and instructional modifications.

Examples of Proposed UbD District Evaluation Studies

Many districts throughout the United States are currently exploring and developing proposals for formal program evaluation studies of Understanding by Design. Three such programs are outlined here to illustrate the range of design features and the rich potential this evaluation process offers. The initiatives underway in the Chancellor's District of the New York City Public Schools; the Conewago Valley School District outside Gettysburg, Pennsylvania; and the San Diego Unified School District, in San Diego, California, each represent multiple years of districtwide UbD training, as well as a systemic commitment to accountability and a determination of the value added by UbD for both student achievement and organizational productivity.

Evaluation Model 1: New York City Public Schools

Our first example involves a proposed multiyear evaluation initiative in New York City. According to Janie Smith, a UbD cadre member from Alexandria, Virginia, who has worked with the district for more than two years to implement UbD, the grant-funded evaluation process will concentrate on selected Title I schools. Smith describes the evaluation design:

> [Its] first priority is to prepare coaches to teach UbD workshops and courses at their school sites during the coming school year [by] providing additional training and materials development time through the following: three days for teaching in the last week of August or early fall, with two to four days [of] ongoing coaching and planning throughout the school year. [We need to] develop training models for courses for credit, ongoing workshops, and professional development days training.

Smith also emphasizes the need for long-term support and advocates expanding the initial focus on language arts and mathematics to include coaches for science, social studies, ESL, and special education.

Like most high-level users, Smith emphasizes that this initiative must more actively include assistant principals and principals in the process of understanding and using UbD.

Smith identifies the following first-year components of the formative evaluation design for participating sites:

> All coaches will submit [an] online UbD unit prior to culmination of [a] year's training. Units will be reviewed to determine the levels of understanding and use without citing designers' names. [Then the following will occur:] Develop questionnaire for coaches, teacher [representatives], and assistant principals to include data gathering on [the] use of UbD in the classroom, workshops, teachers coached, etc. Develop questionnaire for students on differences and characteristics noted in UbD coached classes, their reaction to assignments provided, and progress made. Examine data from coaches' classes, focusing on the number of students who pass the Regents [after having] previously failed, the number of students in cohort group who pass Regents, etc. Collect and review coaches' journal entries on "Use of UbD in My Classroom" to determine comfort level with implementing training. Review and revise training topics and schedule of topics to improve and adjust future trainings as needed. Include some reviewed student work to determine quality of assignments and understandings about topics.

Evaluation Model 2: Conewago Valley School District

This district is in its third year of Understanding by Design implementation. Like New York City's evaluation proposal, Conewago staff members, working with UbD cadre member Elizabeth Rossini from Fairfax, Virginia, emphasize the need to assess levels of staff understanding and use of UbD and its effect on stakeholder performance, including both educators and students. Rossini summarizes the district's proposed evaluation research questions:

> How can we get teachers to implement their units? What support can we provide teachers during the planning and implementation of the units, as well as during the post-unit reflection? How do we maintain discussions around UbD as a curriculum and instructional planning framework? How do we move teachers beyond the required

"one unit per year implementation" to a "way of thinking about planning" that is based on the principles of backward design? What support do administrators need in order to use the principles of UbD in their own work and in support of their teachers doing the same?

Both the New York City and Conewago evaluation proposals integrate long-range continuous improvement and strategic planning related to UbD and its effect on organizational culture. Rossini highlights the following recommended next steps in moving toward institutionalization and in evaluating UbD's effect on the district:

> Provide follow-up and support for teachers. Get teachers to implement units. Publish successes. Analyze feedback from reflective logs, and look for trends, strengths, weaknesses, etc. Share comments, insights, and/or lessons learned from the reflective log. Keep UbD in front of teachers [through] sharing of articles, e-mails, and/or memos with topics to think about or for future discussion in meetings.

In addition to this emphasis on keeping UbD design principles in the forefront of teacher study and inquiry groups, Rossini emphasizes the following for district-level organizational development:

> Use [the] UbD framework for administrative planning. Adopt [and use] the UbD vocabulary . . . to discuss curriculum and instruction. Tie UbD to teacher evaluation. Incorporate UbD into teacher observation in the form of "look fors." Support teachers to come together to refine units based on feedback from implementation. Set up discussion groups for support. Other related training sessions [should include] refining rubrics using actual student work, developing units through the lenses of the six facets of understanding, a deeper look at performance tasks and rubrics, and curriculum mapping your year [on the basis of] Stage One of UbD.

Evaluation Model 3: San Diego Unified School District

Elaine (Irish) Hodges, director of special projects and accountability for the San Diego County Office of Education (SDCOE), San Diego,

California, reinforces a similar systemic commitment to a comprehensive and integrated implementation and evaluation design:

> We started a large project called Standards in Action. The first year of the project, we had 13 districts, 100 teacher leaders, and about 12 SDCOE staff with curriculum and/or process expertise. We met with the teachers about 11 days over a year's time . . . following [with] continued work with the teachers to develop [backward-designed] curriculum units. Along the way, the district curriculum and instruction administrators met together to discuss how they would support the teachers in their districts and [would] further this work in their districts.

Hodges, like all high-level users, emphasizes the issue of follow-through and follow-up feedback as essential to effective UbD implementation and evaluation:

> SDCOE staff worked with the teachers to help facilitate the process and edit the work. As the year ended, we had three binders ([across] grade spans) of the finished units and a CD, and [we] had a workshop to roll them out. The second year of the project, we had Jay [McTighe] come do the kick-off again. This time, we have 16 districts and 50 teachers and many SDCOE staff [members]. We have developed an online process for entering and editing the work. Our eight professional development days have included presentations on each of the stages [of backward design], [differentiated] instruction, and a peer review process.

SDCOE describes its charge in relation to program evaluation thus: "To participate in a professional study of Understanding by Design concepts and create a professional development series for K–12 teachers and administrators in support of standards-based teaching and learning." This process focuses on the following research questions:

• What knowledge and skills do teachers need to design and implement understanding-based lessons and assessment?

- How will the professional development model ensure a focus on academic standards?

- What parameters need to be in place to ensure linkage between professional development and student achievement?

- How will the professional development model and its implementation be evaluated?

- What are the expectations for staff implementation of standards and understanding-based lessons and assessments?

- How will the professional development needs of individual teachers be met?

SDCOE has established three primary purpose, or outcome, statements for its standards-driven initiative of professional development and evaluation: (1) exploring and applying the concepts and principles of UbD, (2) developing reflective practices that support effective problem solving and that improve SDCOE's work, and (3) designing a unit of study to be reviewed by peers and implemented with students. Accompanying "desired outcomes" include shared understanding of UbD concepts and principles, establishment of a professional learning community based on trust and collegiality, and units of study designed around UbD principles.

Finally, SDCOE's UbD users have identified five major "critical success" indicators for implementation and evaluation, each of which is accompanied by a five-point rubric and articulated examples of acceptable evidence:

- *Indicator #1*: Understand and use standards.

- *Indicator #2*: Determine acceptable evidence.

- *Indicator #3*: Design and implement understanding-based lessons.

- *Indicator #4:* Enhance student ownership for learning.

- *Indicator #5:* Use professional collaboration about student learning.

Each of the three evaluation models presented here reflects the range of issues facing a particular school or district, including organizational priorities and student achievement issues. However, each reinforces certain universal patterns that high-level users tend to emphasize. First, representatives of all stakeholder groups must play an active and ongoing part of the evaluation design and implementation process. Second, evaluation standards and performance indicators must be aligned with the priorities articulated in a specific district's long-range plan for continuous improvement. Third, time, money, and human resources must be made available to ensure effective implementation of the proposed plan and its related outcomes. Finally, any effective evaluation plan must reinforce and support overall district accountability goals, thereby generating data to confirm the value that UbD adds as a catalyst for organizational change and renewal.

■ ■ ■

As we conclude this exploration of UbD's relationship to strategic planning and continuous improvement, you may want to refer to Figure 7.1 for a sample of common school or district improvement goals and the corresponding implications for UbD implementation, and to the organizational assessment matrix respresented in Figure 7.2 for a guide to follow-up discussions and explorations. In particular, Figure 7.2 can help you evaluate the extent to which each of 14 interrelated factors that influence organization development, continuous improvement, and strategic planning—from an articulated philosophy of learning, to a consensus-driven commitment, to differentiated instruction that addresses specific strengths and needs of all students—is operational in your school, district, or related learning organization.

7.1	UNDERSTANDING BY DESIGN IMPLICATIONS FOR CONTINUOUS IMPROVEMENT GOALS	

SCHOOL OR DISTRICT GOALS	UNDERSTANDING BY DESIGN IMPLICATIONS
Reinforce school or district commitment to a coherent core curriculum that emphasizes equity and excellence.	Use the three-circle audit process to build consensus about what all students should know, be able to do, and understand.
Ensure that all staff members understand district standards and their implications for high-stakes accountability testing.	Provide UbD training to help teachers and administrators unpack district standards and their implications for required testing.
Reinforce students' understanding of the big ideas and interconnections within the curriculum.	Integrate enduring understandings and essential questions as cueing devices within all curriculum content.
Make certain that all students achieve high levels of understanding, not just formulaic knowledge recall.	Emphasize the six facets of understanding: explanation, interpretation, application, perspective, empathy, and self-knowledge.
Ensure that assessment provides a complete and balanced portrait of what all students know, are able to do, and understand.	Adopt the UbD photo album approach, which integrates constructed-response test items, reflective assessments, academic prompts, and GRASPS culminating projects.
Help students to move along a continuum from concrete to abstract, from teacher-guided to independent learning.	Organize units so that students' learning will spiral toward independent application, including successfully completing GRASPS culminating projects.

Continued

SCHOOL OR DISTRICT GOALS	UNDERSTANDING BY DESIGN IMPLICATIONS
Reinforce all students' sense of efficacy, purpose, and authenticity.	Integrate the "W" (*Where* are we heading, *why* are we going there, and in *what ways* will we be evaluated?) of WHERETO in daily lesson design and delivery.
Engage student interest and ownership.	*Hook* students (the "H" of WHERETO) in key sections of all lessons.
Equip all students for success through *experiential* learning opportunities.	Reinforce the first "E" of WHERETO, emphasizing hands-on inquiry.
Reinforce students' ability to monitor their own comprehension (i.e., metacognition and self-regulation).	Stress the four "Rs" of WHERETO: *reflect, revisit, revise,* and *rethink.*
Encourage students to *exhibit* their understanding, to self-*evaluate,* and to self-express.	Emphasize the second "E" of WHERETO using strategies such as listen-think-pair-share activities, journaling, interviews, and presentations.
Use differentiated instruction to accommodate the strengths and needs of all students.	*Tailor* learning activities (the "T" of WHERETO) to address all students' strengths and needs, including tutorials, coaching, and compacting and acceleration.
Organize instruction to maximize learning for all students, including special populations.	*Organize* learning (the "O" of WHERETO) around big ideas and essential questions, revisiting core knowledge and skills with increasing complexity and independence.

7.2   CONTINUOUS IMPROVEMENT PRINCIPLES AND PRACTICES THAT PROMOTE A COMMUNITY OF LEARNING AND INQUIRY

To what extent does the organizational culture of your school or district reflect each of the following indicators?

INDICATOR	NOT EVIDENT	SOMEWHAT EVIDENT	EVIDENT	HIGHLY EVIDENT
1. We share an articulated philosophy of learning that is consistent with the best in current research-based practice.	☐	☐	☐	☐
2. All changes in curriculum design, including framework documents, evolve from a decision-making process that is consensus-driven.	☐	☐	☐	☐
3. One of our primary institutional values is our commitment to both excellence and equity, thus guaranteeing that all students achieve understanding of our core curriculum.	☐	☐	☐	☐
4. We strive to overcome initiative overload by reinforcing staff members' understanding of the interconnections among our accountability initiatives.	☐	☐	☐	☐

Continued

INDICATOR	NOT EVIDENT	SOMEWHAT EVIDENT	EVIDENT	HIGHLY EVIDENT
5. Our curriculum is a system for managing the learning process, with clear alignment among our written, tested, taught, supported, and learned curricula.	☐	☐	☐	☐
6. Our professional development process supports our commitment to create communities of inquiry and learning.	☐	☐	☐	☐
7. All staff development activities are long term and job embedded, thus emphasizing staff study groups, inquiry teams, and action research cohorts.	☐	☐	☐	☐
8. All stakeholders, including students, parents, and community members, understand and support our vision, mission, and objectives.	☐	☐	☐	☐
9. Continuing assessment and evaluation of programs and initiatives allow us to determine their added value (i.e., their effect on our goals and objectives).	☐	☐	☐	☐

Continued   **Organizational Assessment**

| 7.2 | CONTINUOUS IMPROVEMENT PRINCIPLES AND PRACTICES THAT PROMOTE A COMMUNITY OF LEARNING AND INQUIRY |

To what extent does the organizational culture of your school or district reflect each of the following indicators?

INDICATOR	NOT EVIDENT	SOMEWHAT EVIDENT	EVIDENT	HIGHLY EVIDENT
10. We are committed to continuous improvement as we collect formative and summative performance data to determine how we are doing and how we need to change.	☐	☐	☐	☐
11. Our continuous improvement involves using multiple forms of assessment and evaluation data rather than a snapshot approach.	☐	☐	☐	☐
12. Our organizational improvement emphasizes consensus-driven planning with clear timelines, benchmarks, and adjustments based on emerging data patterns.	☐	☐	☐	☐
13. Instructional leadership involves all personnel in a shared commitment to monitoring and promoting the achievement of all students.	☐	☐	☐	☐

Continued

INDICATOR	NOT EVIDENT	SOMEWHAT EVIDENT	EVIDENT	HIGHLY EVIDENT
14. Our commitment to instructional improvement reflects our willingness to differentiate instruction to meet the strengths and needs of all students, including special populations.	☐	☐	☐	☐

LOOKING TO THE FUTURE OF
UNDERSTANDING BY DESIGN

ESSENTIAL QUESTIONS

1. *How do high-level users perceive the future of Understanding by Design?*

2. *How can educators overcome barriers and pitfalls that are recurrent experiences among most high-level Understanding by Design users?*

3. *How can Understanding by Design support collective efforts to prepare students for success in the change-dominated, technology-driven world of the 21st century?*

Now that we have explored where we have been with Understanding by Design (UbD), let's examine possible future directions and recommendations from high-level users about unpacking its full potential as an educational intervention. When asked about their vision for the future of UbD, most high-level users emphasize the following key focuses:

• The need for an expanded national database of exemplary UbD units and related exemplars involving areas such as revised standards infused with enduring understandings and essential questions.

• The desire to expand the parameters of UbD use to encompass the process of school renewal through strategic planning and continuous improvement, especially as UbD relates to high-stakes accountability initiatives and the promotion of success for all learners.

• A major commitment to expanding UbD's influence to include systemic curriculum development.

• A recurrent recommendation that the linkages between UbD for professional development and other national frameworks be made more overt and clear to educators.

For example, Frank Champine, social studies lead teacher (K–12) in the Neshaminy School District's Department of Curriculum and Instruction in Langhorne, Pennsylvania, states

> I believe UbD will, if developed properly, become the best model for district self-correction. It is simple to learn, it can focus a foundation for curriculum development and instructional practice, and it provides a sound understanding of the role of assessment in individual and district practice. I see UbD becoming the complete model for saving school districts within the confines of the new Bush No Child Left [Behind] plan. It could save districts, if packaged correctly.

In support of this process, Tony Spears, director of curriculum and professional development at the San Diego County Office of Education in San Diego, California, recommends "[the publication of] at least one model unit in the core subjects by grade span (e.g., K–2, 3–5, 6–8, and 9–12), in English–language arts, mathematics, science, and history–social science."

Similarly, Joseph Corriero, assistant superintendent for curriculum and instruction in Cranford, New Jersey, suggests, "It would be helpful to have short how-to videos that focus on specific areas, such as essential questions, alignment issues, [integration of] the six facets of understanding into assessments, etc. We also need more models of exemplary units."

David Malone, senior vice president of Quality Learning in Missouri City, Texas, reinforces the need to expand the UbD electronic learning community: "I see the next level of the UbD Exchange being the ability to create an online interface to be delivered directly to students."

The need for more overt attention to the connection between UbD and standards-based accountability is also a recurrent theme among high-level users. For example, Elliott Seif, a UbD cadre member and a former curriculum developer in Bucks County, Pennsylvania, advocates "focus[ing] more on the connection of UbD to standards. Use UbD as a way to manage and make sense of standards. Also, focus on demonstrating high levels of achievement using UbD. Connect it to curriculum renewal."

According to Lynne Meara, supervisor of instruction and gifted and talented coordinator for the Plumsted Township School District in New Egypt, New Jersey, "Consistency is a vitally important part of any program that is initiated in a school district. The proof will be in both the successful results on student learning, as well as on the continued commitment by staff and administration."

This aspect of high-level users' vision for UbD's future reinforces a commitment to letting the framework become a catalyst for differentiated instruction, particularly for special populations. Deborah Jo Alberti, assistant director of special and gifted education services for the Norfolk Public Schools in Norfolk, Virginia, expresses her hopes for UbD's future in regards to high-ability students:

> Because UbD now actually brings forth for all students many of the approaches formerly associated with gifted programming, I hope to see some effort to build in a way to address differentiation for high-ability learners in the future framework. That said, [finding] a way to address modifications for any learner with special needs would send a loud message that high-quality learning is for all students, but here is a structure to use to "modify" access to this high-quality learning as needed.

Many high-level users align their vision for the future with a caveat: educators must recognize both the inherent complexity of the framework itself and the dissonance that can emerge when old practices conflict with new ones. For example, Linda Marion, a staff development resource teacher from Chula Vista, California, cautions, "This is not something that can be put out in a packet for teachers. It requires a great deal of time and energy to help teachers make such a paradigm shift. It requires the trainer to be a change agent and do a lot of hand holding."

The emerging vision of UbD as a vehicle for organizational renewal and educational reform is also accompanied by high-level users' reinforcement of the need to involve all major stakeholders and to disseminate information about benchmarks and research-based examples of UbD's successful implementation. Margaret Searle, an educational consultant in Perrysburg, Ohio, suggests, "You might think of ways to tell administrators very specific ways to support the process. Where there is a weak or uninformed administrator, there is a lack of support for putting teachers together into networking teams—big trouble with follow through."

Similarly, Mark Wise, a social studies supervisor at Grover Middle School in Princeton Junction, New Jersey, states

> I would suggest that a new model be considered where UbD adopts a school [or] district and commits the time, resources, and energy to fewer schools but deepens the relationship. Once these schools are operating in an exemplary fashion, they could be used by UbD to train other schools or [to] partner them when the next "adoption" takes place. The strength of this work is its simplicity; however, [UbD] takes a lot of work for people to see how simple it is. Getting it right in several schools, I think, would be more useful than having [UbD] exist in pockets in multiple schools.

In general, high-level users gravitate to 10 recommendations for realizing UbD's full potential. Although each idea has power in its own right, together they synthesize how successful educational reform initiatives can become catalysts for ensuring the success of all learners:

1. Develop and implement a comprehensive series of evaluation studies to determine the value that UbD adds in classrooms, schools, and districts that have been using this framework over a sustained period.

2. Publish a synthesis of best practices that have been proven effective in sustaining educators' use of UbD's principles and strategies.

3. Create summaries showing the alignment between UbD and other national and international frameworks and programs such as differentiated instruction, multiple intelligences, learning styles, and constructivist teaching and learning.

4. In both print and electronic formats (e.g., through the UbD Exchange), showcase districts that have integrated enduring understandings and essential questions into their curriculum standards.

5. Greatly expand the availability of models and exemplars of how educators have integrated UbD into their work with special populations (e.g., gifted and talented, special education, ESL, and socio-economically disadvantaged students).

6. Provide clear and practical examples of how UbD can be integrated into continuous improvement initiatives, including school improvement plans and district strategic plans.

7. Expand opportunities for UbD users who have similar jobs to interact and learn from one another through conferences and electronic media sources such as online dialogues and message boards.

8. Create electronic databases with field-tested exemplars of UbD elements such as enduring understandings, essential questions, academic prompts, culminating projects, and hook activities. Although those elements can be found within the units posted on the UbD Exchange, it would be useful to have additional ones posted separately according to content.

9. Expand the emphasis given to UbD work that has been successfully completed with primary students. Many practitioners reinforce the complexity and challenges of integrating teaching for understanding into educators' work with students in the early learning years.

10. Nail down the issue of how Understanding by Design reinforces work with high-stakes accountability testing. In spite of many educators' efforts to the contrary, many schools and districts still have a teach-to-the-test mentality.

Aligning Understanding with Other National Professional Development Frameworks and Programs

One major issue many high-level users cite is the need to help educators understand connections and linkages among the numerous professional and organizational development initiatives operating today. Two frameworks are frequently cited as having close alignment with UbD and its core principles and strategies. The first framework is What Works in Schools, articulated by Robert J. Marzano in *What Works in Schools: Translating Research into Action* (2003). The second framework is differentiated instruction, as presented by Carol Ann Tomlinson in *The Differentiated Classroom* (1999).

The Marzano connection extends from practitioners' desire for a more overt articulation and dissemination of the educational research base underlying the Wiggins and McTighe model. Similarly, the frequent allusions to Tomlinson's concept of differentiated instruction reinforce practitioners' shared concern about how to successfully address the needs of increasingly diverse student populations. Briefly, all three frameworks share the following common values and principles:

• A commitment to fostering high levels of achievement for all learners through an education dedicated to rigor, excellence, and equity.

• A recognition that learning requires a high level of motivation and commitment on the part of the student, which can be fostered by authentic and learner-centered instruction.

• An acknowledgment that a carefully articulated and consensus-driven curriculum emphasizing high standards for all learners is a non-negotiable requirement for a successful education.

• The assertion that instruction and assessment must be consistently interconnected, with formative and summative assessment data used to monitor student learning and to adjust instruction that will accommodate emerging strengths and needs.

• The shared recognition of the learner as the center of the learning process, including the need for educators to address students' learning style preferences, personal interests, and readiness levels when designing and delivering instruction.

UbD and What Works in Schools

Understanding by Design reflects many of the research-based conclusions and recommendations in Marzano (2003). Presenting evidence from his analysis of educational research over the past 35 years, Marzano synthesizes the recurrent practices that make successful schools successful and presents them in three categories: school-level factors, teacher-level factors, and student-level factors. His school-level factors include the need for a guaranteed and viable curriculum, a set of challenging goals and effective feedback, parental and community involvement, a safe and orderly environment, and a sense of collegiality and professionalism. Marzano's teacher-level factors, based on the practices of teachers who promote high levels of student performance, include the need to use a range of research-based instructional strategies, manage classrooms through clearly articulated and student-owned policies and procedures, and design curriculum in alignment with consensus-driven standards. Finally, there are the student-level factors. Learners contribute to educational achievement when they have an enriched and supportive home environment, a clear sense of their own motivation and how they can improve it, and an extensive background knowledge resulting from enrichment experiences and ongoing involvement in wide reading and vocabulary development.

UbD provides strategies and processes for implementing many of Marzano's recommendations. While high-level users argue for viewing the Wiggins and McTighe framework as a model for reform at the district or systemic level, the following requirements for educational renewal are immediate and obvious areas of direct alignment between UbD and What Works in Schools:

• *Ensure a guaranteed and viable curriculum that identifies core content and ensures sufficient time for students to learn it.* For this factor, the three-circle audit process provides an ideal technology to build consensus about curriculum content, thus helping staffs to distinguish between what is worth just being familiar with versus what all students should know, be able to do, and understand.

• *Establish challenging goals and provide effective feedback for all learners.* UbD reinforces the need for all students to develop deep conceptual understanding through experience-based inquiry into enduring understandings and essential questions, as well as demonstration of independent mastery through the six facets of understanding.

• *Ensure that all students learn within a safe and orderly environment.* Marzano's emphasis on clear rules and procedures to promote good behavior and to minimize disruption to the learning process is complemented by UbD's insistence on students' being at the center of their own learning process. By encouraging self-knowledge and self-reflection, educators help students to experience their education as being authentic and clearly connected to their world.

• *Reinforce a school culture reflective of collegiality and professionalism.*
Marzano (2003) emphasizes the power of collaboration and shared
inquiry in all facets of school operations. UbD emphasizes lesson study
and unit evaluation using the peer review process. UbD confirms that
professional understanding of the framework is a collaborative, not an
individual, process and contributes to an overall school culture that is
positive and inviting for all stakeholders.

• *Provide instruction that reflects research-based best practices.* Marzano (2003) identifies nine areas of pedagogical practice that have a
high statistical effect relative to student achievement: (1) identifying
similarities and differences; (2) summarizing and note taking; (3) reinforcing effort and providing recognition; (4) extending and refining
student learning through homework and practice; (5) using nonlinguistic representations of information; (6) using cooperative learning;
(7) setting clear objectives and coaching-based feedback that are tied
to standards criteria; (8) generating and testing hypotheses; and (9)
using cues, higher-order questions, and advance organizers. All these
strategies and practices are implicit and explicit in UbD's emphasis on
the big ideas, the essential questions, the GRASPS concepts and
related independent performance tasks, the six facets of understanding,
and the WHERETO template.

• *Implement effective classroom management strategies and processes.*
The contention that rules, policies, and classroom management techniques can contribute significantly to students' ownership of the learning process is at the heart of Marzano's research analysis. UbD
reinforces effective classroom management by empowering students to
be responsible for their own progress, to be self-regulated and self-
aware, and to move toward independent use of knowledge wherever
possible. It is the student, not the teacher, who is responsible for his or
her own progress, with appropriate intervention and coaching from the
teacher as facilitator.

• *Ensure that classroom curriculum design is standards driven, clearly and coherently designed and presented, and engaging for students.* Both the Marzano (2003) research synthesis and UbD emphasize the following design elements: (1) specification and communication of an essential and time-sensitive set of rigorous standards for all learners; (2) use of various instructional modalities and a commitment to revisiting core learnings in many ways throughout a student's education; (3) conceptual organization of curriculum content to highlight the essential features of its content areas, including emphasis on big ideas, essential questions, and enduring understandings; (4) involvement of students in complex projects that require them to address content in special ways; and (5) emphasis on student efficacy through self-knowledge and metacognition.

• *Acknowledge that all students are capable of developing deep understanding and conceptual mastery by emphasizing their development of learned intelligence and background knowledge.* What Works in Schools and Understanding by Design both reinforce the idea that all learners can study and learn a rigorous, conceptually organized core curriculum if their education (1) directly increases the number and quality of life experiences they have; (2) engages them in wide reading and vocabulary development; and (3) reinforces their conceptual understanding, rather than their ability to repeat information formulaically.

• *Increase student motivation by providing a learning environment that provides meaningful and ongoing feedback.* Both frameworks emphasize coaching-based feedback that includes opportunities for students to understand how they are progressing toward standards acquisition and understanding, as well as cooperative learning-based options for peer coaching and feedback, including peer response groups.

• *Enhance student motivation by engaging learners in independent projects and activities that promote self-knowledge.* Explicit in both What

Works in Schools and Understanding by Design is the recognition that the more learners are responsible for their own learning process and its related results, the greater their innate motivation. Both frameworks, therefore, encourage educators to engage students in simulations, performance-based tasks, and culminating projects that allow for student choice, design, and self-monitoring whenever possible.

UbD and Differentiated Instruction

Like Marzano's research-based framework and Wiggins and McTighe's Understanding by Design, Tomlinson's work with differentiated instruction reinforces the need for a learner-centered educational process that accommodates student strengths and needs. Similarly, all three frameworks reinforce the close link between assessment and instruction, with the assertion that teachers are always engaged in a process of monitoring and assessing student performance and, in turn, making appropriate instructional adjustments to accommodate data-based needs and issues.

In her best-selling book *The Differentiated Classroom* (1999), Tomlinson presents a model for teaching that strikingly parallels many of Marzano's and Wiggins and McTighe's recommendations. Specifically, she suggests that differentiated instruction represents a teacher's response to the learner's needs. This response is guided by three general principles: (1) ongoing assessment and adjustment; (2) flexible grouping; and (3) respectful tasks, which consider the readiness level of each student, expect all students to grow, offer all students the opportunity to explore enduring understandings and skills at escalating rates of difficulty and proficiency, and offer all students tasks that look—and are—equally interesting, equally important, and equally engaging (Tomlinson, 1999, p. 12). Tomlinson also contends that teachers can differentiate curriculum content, instructional and learning processes, and products according to students' individual readiness, interests, and learning profile.

Like the other two frameworks, Tomlinson's recommendations for instructional and management strategies address multiple learning modalities; reinforce big ideas and conceptual understandings; and allow for individual student choice through tools such as learning contracts, tiered lessons, learning centers, independent and group investigations, varied questioning techniques, and various student self-assessment and self-reflection tools.

Understanding by Design reinforces most of Tomlinson's recommendations for differentiated instruction to ensure maximum learning for all students. The following represent the most overt connections between the two frameworks:

• *Respond directly and continually to individual students' needs through ongoing assessment and adjustment.* UbD addresses this component of differentiation by emphasizing the teacher's need to articulate clearly the objectives, understandings, and questions that will guide students' inquiry and learning process within the lesson, unit, and course or grade level. It emphasizes the close relationship among assessment, instruction, and learning, with the teacher continually monitoring and responding to students' expressed strengths and needs.

• *Ensure that all students participate in respectful work.* Once again, Understanding by Design—like Tomlinson's model of differentiated instruction—asserts that enduring understandings and competencies should be goals for all students. Using a photo album approach to assessment (combining tests and quizzes with constructed-response items, reflective assessments, academic prompts, and GRASPS culminating projects), the teacher constantly assesses and adjusts the instruction and learning process. The identity of the individual is at the heart of assessing and teaching for understanding, with the learner engaging in increasingly complex and challenging tasks that promote growing levels of conceptual understanding and independent application.

• *Differentiate according to curriculum content, process, and product, based on students' readiness, interests, and learning profiles.* UbD's photo album approach for a balanced and multifaceted assessment aligns with its WHERETO instructional template (see Chapter 1, page 19) to address these factors of differentiation.

• *Use a range of instructional and management strategies to reinforce success for all students.* Both the Tomlinson framework and the UbD framework stress acknowledging and addressing students as individuals with unique learning profiles and individual ways of manifesting their intelligence. Tailoring, the "T" element in WHERETO, resonates with Tomlinson's long list of recommended differentiation techniques. Those techniques include cooperative learning structures; varied texts and resources; tiered lessons and learning contracts; independent and group investigations; interest groups and centers; journaling; and curriculum compacting. This last technique involves assessing students' levels of knowledge and skills relative to unit standards and allowing students with pre-existing mastery to move toward more independent work, while those requiring additional direct instruction participate in some form of tutorial or coaching experiences.

These three frameworks and their multiple areas of alignment reinforce an emergent theme in this study of high-level users: the growing consensus within contemporary education about what we need to do and how we need to do it so that we may help all students succeed. The very real and profound connections evident in these models also reinforce high-level users' expressed commitment to aligning district efforts to improve student achievement and to overcome the phenomenon of educational reform as a series of isolated, stand-alone programs and practices.

Shared Vision Statements for the Future of Education and Understanding by Design

This final section presents a series of statements that reflect study participants' recommendations for several major areas of educational reform. The statements represent both a shared vision for UbD and its application to the learning organization, as well as high-level users' hopes and aspirations for educational practice in the new millennium.

Student Achievement

All students develop a deep conceptual understanding of the curriculum they study. They gain a clear and sustained ability to confirm that understanding through one or more of the six facets of understanding: explanation, interpretation, application, perspective, empathy, and self-knowledge. Through backward design, educators accommodate the unique strengths and needs of all learners, thus ensuring their academic success and their sense of personal efficacy and self-regulation. The needs of all students—including those representing special populations—are addressed appropriately and consistently.

Curriculum Standards

All schools and districts have consensus-driven curriculum standards that are designed to promote understanding for all. Through these standards, learning organizations ensure that they have an effective system for monitoring student progress through content standards that are relevant, challenging, and rigorous for all learners. Content standards are complemented by performance standards and benchmarks that allow for feedback and adjustment of instruction within each marking or grading period.

Curriculum Design

All curriculum documents (including scope, sequence, and related cur-riculum frameworks, as well as curriculum guides) provide clear and coherent road maps for instructors to ensure that all students master identified district standards. Curricula model the essential UbD prin-ciples, including a viable core curriculum (arrived at through the three-circle audit process) that emphasizes enduring understand-ings and essential questions, the six facets of understanding, a photo album of assessment strategies, and the WHERETO instructional design template.

Assessment and Program Evaluation

All educators within each school and district understand and use a consensus-driven assessment and evaluation process to monitor stu-dent achievement. This process emphasizes a clear alignment between identified content and performance standards, plus related assessment tools and techniques. All teachers use a photo album of assessment processes, just as all districts use a photo album approach to evaluate school performance and progress. Standardized testing represents only one component of the total process for evaluating student achieve-ment and organizational effectiveness.

Instructional Design and Delivery

All schools and districts ensure that adequate time and resources are available for teachers to implement the core curriculum in a manner that ensures the achievement of all learners. Every teacher consistently addresses the following essential questions: *Where* are we headed, *why* are we going there, and in *what ways* will we be evaluated along the way? How will student interest and sense of purpose be *hooked* in all units and lessons? How will all students be *equipped* for success through *experience*-based learning activities? How will all students be supported to *reflect, revisit, revise,* and *rethink* their learning? How will students be empowered to *exhibit* self-expression and *self-evaluation*? How will we *tailor* instruction to address the unique strengths and needs of all learners? How will we *organize* instruction so that all students move from experience and exploration toward deep conceptual understanding and independent application?

Professional Development

All educators within a district, from teachers to administrators to paraprofessionals, participate in meaningful and sustained professional development to ensure that they acquire the skills, competencies, and understandings needed to promote the success of all learners. Professional development is sensitive to the needs of all adult learners, is aligned with site-based concerns and needs, and incorporates a variety of reflective practices, including study groups and action research cohorts. All schools and districts have a viable program evaluation process in place to determine the value that staff development activities and programs add, particularly how they affect student understanding and overall achievement.

Administration and School Leadership

All administrators within a school or district model the characteristics of genuine instructional leadership. They facilitate staff understanding and promote shared inquiry and an overall community of inquiry and learning. Through their coaching, observation, and related feedback practices, administrators promote the idea of staff members as lifelong learners committed to the continuous improvement of student achievement relative to consensus-driven district standards. Administrators ensure that teacher leadership is an evident, significant, and sustained variable in their school's or district's approach to instructional leadership. Administrators are far more than managers: they are active catalysts in facilitating staff and student understanding.

Models for Supervision

Antiquated models of supervision as externalized management are replaced by supervisors as cognitive coaches and facilitators of staff understanding and professional growth. Supervisory personnel are active participants in the school and district learning community, committed to promoting all students' success and understanding. Supervisors ensure that the educators they work with receive support and purposeful feedback that enhances their ability to understand and implement the principles of backward design in their respective professional practices, including determination of clear and ambitious desired results, implementation of a viable assessment and evaluation process to monitor those results, and a delivery system to maximize overall achievement of articulated results.

Strategic Planning and Continuous Improvement

All schools and districts ensure the mastery of identified standards by all students. Long- and short-term results for student, staff, and organizational performance are consensus driven and rigorous. Staff members work collaboratively to understand those results and to develop and implement effective action plans to ensure their achievement. Formative and summative assessment and evaluation data are generated and analyzed in a timely fashion, with data-based decision making used to design, implement, and adjust educational programs and practices. The strategic plan used by a school, district, or related learning organization is not an exercise on paper, but an organic, ever-changing road map to promote and sustain achievement throughout the learning organization. Strategic planning and continuous improvement processes are differentiated to ensure that the needs and strengths of all stakeholders are accommodated. Parents, community members, and students—like all staff members—clearly understand the purpose of this process and are active participants in it.

Parent and Community Outreach

All parents and community members understand the standards, the assessment and evaluation processes, and the instructional delivery systems advocated by their school and district. They receive sustained encouragement to play an active role in school governance, including problem-solving and decision-making processes that address and ensure the achievement of all learners. Parents and community members support the principles and practices of teaching for understanding. They work actively with school and district officials to ensure that time, material, and human resources are available to support the achievement of all learners within a school or district committed to promoting understanding, not just knowledge–recall learning.

District and State Leadership, Including Boards of Education

District leaders, including members of Boards of Education and related governance authorities, as well as state Boards and Departments of Education, support the principles of the backward design process. They work collaboratively to ensure that required resources are available so that all staff members may promote the understanding and achievement of all students. Like school-based and central office personnel, the district- and state-level leaders understand and actively support a consensus-driven curriculum that is designed to promote the understanding and engagement of all students. They also support the concept of a balanced, photo album approach to assessment and evaluation, complemented by an instructional delivery system that models WHERETO principles and strategies. They are part of an active community of learning, which avoids "gotcha" practices and an unbalanced or excessive emphasis on test scores as the most important criterion for judging school effectiveness.

Together, these vision statements represent the high-level users' perspectives and hopes for the future. Although idealistic on the surface, such statements express a shared commitment to the possibility of genuinely transforming education from the existing antiquated industrial models and paradigms to the concept of schools and districts as true learning organizations. In effect, respondents agree, the use of frameworks such as UbD can provide a language and a set of controlling principles to guide educational reform and renewal in this era of rising expectations and diminishing resources.

■   ■   ■

Our journey concludes with Figure 8.1's organizational assessment, based on a summary of the major recommendations for the future of education from the perspective of high-level UbD users. You may wish to reflect on each inference and its implications for education in the new millennium. You and your fellow educators are encouraged to collaborate on an organizational examination of your school or district and of where it stands in relation to each of the 20 identified factors. Ideally, Understanding by Design can support you in ensuring that no child is ever left behind and that all students develop deep conceptual understanding and a lifelong commitment to learning.

8.1   A VISION FOR SCHOOLING THAT PROMOTES UNDERSTANDING FOR ALL AND A LIFELONG COMMITMENT TO LEARNING

To what extent does the vision for the future of education in your school or district reflect each of the following indicators?

INDICATOR	NOT EVIDENT	SOMEWHAT EVIDENT	EVIDENT	HIGHLY EVIDENT
1. Our vision and mission emphasize our commitment to helping all students achieve deep understanding of our curriculum.	☐	☐	☐	☐
2. Our learning organization consistently reflects the best of what we now know about the learning process.	☐	☐	☐	☐
3. We offer a curriculum that is clearly articulated, with standards that promote understanding for all.	☐	☐	☐	☐
4. We consistently design our curriculum to ensure that it identifies the big ideas, enduring understandings, and essential questions critical for student understanding.	☐	☐	☐	☐
5. Our curriculum emphasizes what all students should know, be able to do, and understand.	☐	☐	☐	☐

Continued   **Organizational Assessment**

8.1   A VISION FOR SCHOOLING THAT PROMOTES UNDERSTANDING FOR ALL AND A LIFELONG COMMITMENT TO LEARNING

To what extent does the vision for the future of education in your school or district reflect each of the following indicators?

INDICATOR	NOT EVIDENT	SOMEWHAT EVIDENT	EVIDENT	HIGHLY EVIDENT
6. We structure our written curriculum to ensure that teachers and students have the time and resources to explore it in depth.	☐	☐	☐	☐
7. Our curriculum management reinforces alignment between and among our written, tested, taught, supported, and learned curricula.	☐	☐	☐	☐
8. Our assessment and evaluation process emphasizes multiple formats to capture the full range of student understanding and performance.	☐	☐	☐	☐
9. All teachers effectively use multiple assessment and evaluation tools for monitoring student understanding and achievement.	☐	☐	☐	☐
10. Our assessment and evaluation process emphasizes identifying and addressing students' strengths and needs relative to their understanding of our curriculum and its standards.	☐	☐	☐	☐

Continued

Indicator	Not Evident	Somewhat Evident	Evident	Highly Evident
11. Teachers use differentiated instruction to accommodate the strengths and needs of students, as identified by our assessment and evaluation process.	☐	☐	☐	☐
12. Instruction ensures that all students understand where they are headed, why they are going there, and in what ways they will be evaluated.	☐	☐	☐	☐
13. At key points in every instructional episode, students' interest and engagement are hooked through experiential activities and inquiry-based learning opportunities.	☐	☐	☐	☐
14. All students are equipped for success through learning experiences that help them explore big ideas and essential questions.	☐	☐	☐	☐
15. Teachers design learning activities to equip all students for success on final culminating projects and related performance tasks.	☐	☐	☐	☐

| *Continued* | **Organizational Assessment** |

| **8.1** | A VISION FOR SCHOOLING THAT PROMOTES UNDERSTANDING FOR ALL AND A LIFELONG COMMITMENT TO LEARNING |

To what extent does the vision for the future of education in your school or district reflect each of the following indicators?

INDICATOR	NOT EVIDENT	SOMEWHAT EVIDENT	EVIDENT	HIGHLY EVIDENT
16. Instruction equips all students to move from concrete experiences toward abstract conceptualization and understanding.	☐	☐	☐	☐
17. As a result of our organizational commitment to the values of reflecting, revisiting, revising, and rethinking, all students are self-aware and self-evaluative.	☐	☐	☐	☐
18. All students exhibit their evolving understanding and mastery of standards through final performances and products.	☐	☐	☐	☐
19. All instructional and professional development activities are tailored to reflect the backward design process: determining desired results (Stage One), monitoring and assessing achievement of desired results (Stage Two), and designing learning activities to promote desired results (Stage Three).	☐	☐	☐	☐

Continued

INDICATOR	NOT EVIDENT	SOMEWHAT EVIDENT	EVIDENT	HIGHLY EVIDENT
20. Our learning approach is organized to reinforce the six facets of understanding: explanation, interpretation, application, perspective, empathy, and self-knowledge.	☐	☐	☐	☐

Appendix A

■ ■ ■

EDUCATORS CITED IN TEXT

Deborah Jo Alberti, Assistant Director of Special and Gifted Education Services, Norfolk Public Schools, Norfolk, Virginia

Alyce Anderson, Principal, Herbertsville Elementary School, Brick, New Jersey

Scott Berger, 8th Grade Social Studies Teacher, Grover Middle School, Princeton Junction, New Jersey

Frank Champine, Social Studies Lead Teacher, K–12, Neshaminy School District, Department of Curriculum and Instruction, Langhorne, Pennsylvania

Joseph Corriero, Assistant Superintendent for Curriculum and Instruction, Cranford, New Jersey

Patty Isabel Cortez, English Language Arts Coach, Morris High School, Bronx, New York

Marnie Dratch, 6th Grade Language Arts Teacher, Grover Middle School, Princeton Junction, New Jersey

Kay Egan, Senior Coordinator for Special and Gifted Education Services, Norfolk Public Schools, Norfolk, Virginia

Judith Hilton, Understanding by Design Cadre Member and University Professor, Greenwood Village, Colorado

Elaine (Irish) Hodges, Director of Special Projects and Accountability, San Diego County Office of Education, San Diego, California

Michael Jackson, 8th Grade Language Arts Teacher, Grover Middle School, Princeton Junction, New Jersey

Dorothy C. Katauskas, Assistant to the Superintendent for Curriculum, Instruction, and Staff Development (K–12), New Hope–Solebury School District, New Hope, Pennsylvania

Jill Levine, Principal, Normal Park Museum Magnet School, Chattanooga, Tennessee

David Malone, Senior Vice President, Quality Learning, Missouri City, Texas

Linda Marion, Staff Development Resource Teacher, Chula Vista, California

Lynne Meara, Supervisor of Instruction and Gifted and Talented Coordinator, Plumsted Township School District, New Egypt, New Jersey

Ken O'Connor, Understanding by Design Cadre Member, Scarborough, Ontario, Canada

Elizabeth Rossini, Understanding by Design Cadre Member, Fairfax, Virginia

Angela Ryan, Instructional Facilitator, Hershey, Pennsylvania

Margaret Searle, Educational Consultant, Perrysburg, Ohio

Elliott Seif, Understanding by Design Cadre Member, Philadelphia, Pennsylvania

Janie Smith, Understanding by Design Cadre Member, Alexandria, Virginia

Judy Solovey, Curriculum Facilitator, Normal Park Museum Magnet School, Chattanooga, Tennessee

Tony Spears, Director of Curriculum and Professional Development, San Diego County Office of Education, San Diego, California

Joan Spratley, Director of Special and Gifted Education, Norfolk Public Schools, Norfolk, Virginia

Joyce Tatum, Understanding by Design Cadre Member and Museum Liaison, Normal Park Museum Magnet School, Chattanooga, Tennessee

Mark Wise, Social Studies Supervisor, Grover Middle School, Princeton Junction, New Jersey

Carl Zon, Standards and Assessment Coach and Educational Consultant, Sunnyvale, California

Jan Zuehlke, Social Studies Coordinator, Willis, Texas

Appendix B

■ ■ ■

LOCATIONS OF FOCUS GROUP SESSIONS

Chancellor's District, New York City Public Schools, New York, New York

Conewago Valley School District, Gettysburg, Pennsylvania

Georgetown Public Schools, Georgetown, South Carolina

Laredo Independent School District, Laredo, Texas

Modesto City School District, Modesto, California

Norfolk Public Schools, Norfolk, Virginia

Orange County Unified School District, Santa Ana, California

San Diego Unified School District, San Diego, California

References and
Resources

Blythe, T., & Associates. (1998). *The teaching for understanding guide*. San Francisco: Jossey-Bass.

Bransford, J. D., Brown, A. L., & Cocking, R. R. (Eds.). (1999). *How people learn: Brain, mind, experience, and school*. Washington, DC: National Academy Press.

Bruner, J. (1996). *The culture of education*. Cambridge, MA: Harvard University Press.

Cohen, F. (2003, May). Mining data to improve teaching: Data warehousing technology gives schools the power to make credible connections between student test scores and teacher effectiveness. *Educational Leadership, 60*(8), 53–56.

Darling-Hammond, L. (2003, May). Keeping good teachers: Why it matters, what leaders can do. *Educational Leadership, 60*(8), 6–13.

Elliott, J. (1991). *Action research for educational change*. Philadelphia: Open University Press.

Erickson, L. (1998). *Concept-based curriculum and instruction: Teaching beyond the facts*. Thousand Oaks, CA: Corwin Press.

Feiman-Nemser, S. (2003, May). What new teachers need to learn: Addressing the learning needs of new teachers can improve both the rate of teacher retention and the quality of the teaching profession. *Educational Leadership, 60*(8), 25–29.

Guskey, T. R. (2002, March). Does it make a difference? Evaluating professional development. *Educational Leadership, 59*(6), 45–51.

Hord, S. M., Rutherford, W. L., Huling-Austin, L., & Hall, G. E. (1987). *Taking care of change*. Alexandria, VA: Association for Supervision and Curriculum Development.

Jacobs, H. H. (1997). *Mapping the big picture: Integrating curriculum and assessment K–12*. Alexandria, VA: Association for Supervision and Curriculum Development.

Joyce, B., Wolf, J., & Calhoun, E. (1993). *The self-renewing school*. Alexandria, VA: Association for Supervision and Curriculum Development.

Kruse, S. D. (1999, Summer). Collaborate. *Journal of Staff Development, 20*(3), 14–16.

Levine, M. (2002, March). Why invest in professional development schools? *Educational Leadership, 59*(6), 65–67.

Lieberman, A., & Miller, L. (1999). *Teachers: Transforming their world and their work*. New York: Teachers College Press.

Marzano, R. J. (1992). *A different kind of classroom: Teaching with Dimensions of Learning*. Alexandria, VA: Association for Supervision and Curriculum Development.

Marzano, R. J. (1998). *A theory-based meta-analysis of research on instruction*. Aurora, CO: Mid-continent Research for Education and Learning. (ERIC Document Reproduction Service No. ED 427087)

Marzano, R. J. (2003). *What works in schools: Translating research into action*. Alexandria, VA: Association for Supervision and Curriculum Development.

Marzano, R. J., & Pickering, D. J. (2001). *Assessing student performance using Dimensions of Learning*. Alexandria, VA: Association for Supervision and Curriculum.

Marzano, R. J., Pickering, D. J., & McTighe, J. (1993). *Assessing student outcomes: Performance assessment using the Dimensions of Learning model*. Alexandria, VA: Association for Supervision and Curriculum Development.

Marzano, R. J., Pickering, D. J., & Pollock, J. E. (2001). *Classroom instruction that works: Research-based strategies for increasing student achievement*. Alexandria, VA: Association for Supervision and Curriculum Development.

McLean, J. E. (1995). *Improving education through action research: A guide for administrators and teachers*. Thousand Oaks, CA: Corwin Press.

McTighe, J. (1996, December–1997, January). What happens between assessments? *Educational Leadership, 54*(4), 6–12.

McTighe, J., & Wiggins, G. (1999). *The Understanding by Design handbook*. Alexandria, VA: Association for Supervision and Curriculum Development.

McTighe, J., & Wiggins, G. (2000). *"Understanding by Design" study guide*. Alexandria, VA: Association for Supervision and Curriculum Development.

McTighe, J., & Wiggins, G. (2004). *The Understanding by Design professional workbook*. Alexandria, VA: Association for Supervision and Curriculum Development.

Moir, E., & Bloom, G. (2003, May). Fostering leadership through mentoring: At the Santa Cruz New Teacher Center, a comprehensive induction program for novices has also reinvigorated veteran teachers and created a new generation of school leaders. *Educational Leadership, 60*(8), 25–29.

Murphy, C. U. (1999, Summer). Study groups. *Journal of Staff Development, 20*(3), 49–51.

Newmann, F. N., & Associates. (1997). *Authentic achievement: Restructuring schools for intellectual quality*. San Francisco: Jossey-Bass.

Newmann, F. N., Secada, W. G., & Wehlage, G. G. (1995). *A guide to authentic instruction and assessment: Vision, standards, and scoring*. Madison, WI: Wisconsin Center for Education Research.

Perkins, D. (1991, October). Educating for insight. *Educational Leadership, 49*(2), 4–8.

Perkins, D. (1992). *Smart schools: From training memories to educating minds*. New York: Free Press.

Robbins, P. (1999, Summer). Mentoring. *Journal of Staff Development, 20*(3), 40–42.

Sagor, R. (1992). *How to conduct collaborative action research*. Alexandria, VA: Association for Supervision and Curriculum Development.

Schmoker, M. (1996). *Results: The key to continuous school improvement*. Alexandria, VA: Association for Supervision and Curriculum Development.

Senge, P. M. (1990). *The fifth discipline: The art and practice of the learning organization*. New York: Doubleday/Currency.

Sheive, L. T., & Schoenheit, M. B. (Eds.). (1987). *Leadership: Examining the elusive—1987 Yearbook of the Association for Supervision and Curriculum Development*. Alexandria, VA: Association for Supervision and Curriculum Development.

Slavin, R. E. (1983). *Cooperative learning*. New York: Longmann.

Smith, W. F., & Andrews, R. L. (1989). *Instructional leadership: How principals make a difference*. Alexandria, VA: Association for Supervision and Curriculum Development.

Sparks, D. (1999, Summer). Interview with Susan Loucks-Horsley: Try on strategies to get a good fit. *Journal of Staff Development, 20*(3), 56–60.

Sparks, D., & Hirsh, S. (1997). *A new vision of staff development.* Alexandria, VA: Association for Supervision and Curriculum Development; and Oxford, OH: National Staff Development Council.

Teddlie, C., & Reynolds, D. (Eds.). (2000). *The international handbook of school effectiveness research.* New York: Falmer Press.

Tomlinson, C. A. (1999). *The differentiated classroom: Responding to the needs of all learners.* Alexandria, VA: Association for Supervision and Curriculum Development.

Wang, M. C., Haertel, G. D., & Walberg, H. J. (1993). Toward a knowledge base for school learning. *Review of Educational Research, 63*(3), 249–294.

Wiggins, G. (1998). *Educative assessment: Designing assessments to inform and improve performance.* San Francisco: Jossey-Bass.

Wiggins, G., & McTighe, J. (1998). *Understanding by design.* Alexandria, VA: Association for Supervision and Curriculum Development.

Willis, S. (2002, March). Creating a knowledge base for teaching: A conversation with James Stigler. *Educational Leadership, 59*(6), 611.

Wiske, M. S. (1997). *Teaching for understanding: Linking research with practice.* San Francisco: Jossey-Bass.

Wong, H. K. (2002, March). Induction: The best form of professional development. *Educational Leadership, 59*(6), 52–54.

Wood, F. H., & McQuarrie, F., Jr. (1999, Summer). On-the-job learning. *Journal of Staff Development, 20*(3), 10–13.

INDEX

ABOUT THE AUTHOR

John L. Brown is an educational consultant for ASCD, where he works with product and professional development and serves as a member of the national training cadres for Understanding by Design and What Works in Schools. He is a former Director of Staff Development and Program Development in Prince George's County Public Schools, Maryland, where he also served as Supervisor of the University High School Magnet Program. He has professional experience in the areas of gifted and talented education and English language arts.

Brown has published extensively, including such ASCD publications as *Observing Dimensions of Learning in Classrooms and Schools* (1995) and *The Hero's Journey: How Educators Can Transform Schools and Improve Learning* (1999) with Cerylle A. Moffett. He has written five ASCD Professional Development Online courses, including a three-part series on Understanding by Design. Brown received his Ph.D. from George Mason University and his M.A. and B.A. from the University of Wisconsin, Madison. He can be reached at jbrown @ascd.org.

Related ASCD Resources: Understanding by Design

At the time of publication, the following ASCD resources were available; for the most up-to-date information about ASCD resources, go to http://www.ascd.org. ASCD stock numbers are noted in parentheses.

Audiotapes

Applying Understanding by Design to School Improvement Planning by Jay McTighe and Ronald S. Thomas (#202143)

Understanding by Design and Differentiated Instruction: Partners in Classroom Success by Grant Wiggins, Jay McTighe, and Carol Ann Tomlinson (#203188)

Understanding by Design: Structures and Strategies for Designing School Reform by Jay McTighe and Grant Wiggins (#202189)

What Does Understanding by Design Have to Do with Professional Development? by Harolyn Katherman and others (#202137)

Online Courses

Register for these courses at http://www.ascd.org or by calling the ASCD Service Center

Understanding by Design: An Introduction

Understanding by Design: Six Facets of Understanding

Understanding by Design: The Backward Design Process

Print Products

Understanding by Design by Grant Wiggins and Jay McTighe (#198199)

The Understanding by Design Handbook by Jay McTighe and Grant Wiggins (#199030)

The Understanding by Design Professional Workbook by Grant Wiggins and Jay McTighe (#103056)

Training

The ASCD Understanding by Design Faculty: ASCD will arrange for a UbD expert to deliver onsite training tailored to the needs of your school, district, or regional service agency. Call (703) 678-9600, ext. 5677.

Videotapes

The Understanding by Design Video Series (3-tape series with facilitator's guide) (#400241)

Web Products

Professional Development Online, at http://www.ascd.org/framepdonline.html features several UbD-related online study courses.

The UbD Exchange, at http://www.ubdexhchange.org, features a database of units designed using the Understanding by Design framework. Try a demo of the UbD Exchange at http://www.ubdexchange.org/demo.html and see how this interactive tool provides feedback for teachers on curriculum and assessment design.

For additional resources, visit us on the World Wide Web (http://www.ascd.org), send an e-mail message to member@ascd.org, call the ASCD Service Center (1-800-933-ASCD or 703-578-9600, then press 2), send a fax to 703-575-5400, or write to Information Services, ASCD, 1703 N. Beauregard St., Alexandria, VA 22311-1714 USA.